AMERICAN MUSEUM OF NATURAL HISTORY

PEOPLES OF
THE PHILIPPINES

D1785790

By A. L. KROEBER

PROFESSOR OF ANTHROPOLOGY, UNIVERSITY OF CALIFORNIA

HANDBOOK SERIES No. 8
SECOND AND REVISED EDITION
SECOND PRINTING

GREENWOOD PRESS, PUBLISHERS
WESTPORT, CONNECTICUT

Library of Congress Cataloging in Publication Data

Kroeber, Alfred Louis, 1876-1960.
   Peoples of the Philippines.

   Reprint of the 1928 ed. published by the American
Museum of Natural History, New York, which was issued as
the 2d ed. of its Handbook series, no. 8.
   Bibliography: p.
   1. Ethnology--Philippine Islands. 2. Philippine
Islands. I. Title. II. Series: American Museum
of Natural History, New York. Handbook series, no. 8.
DS665.K7   1973   915.99'03'32   73-10850
ISBN 0-8371-7040-0

PUBLICATION

OF THE

ANTHROPOLOGICAL HANDBOOK FUND

DS
665
K7
1974

Originally published in 1928 by the American Museum of
Natural History, New York

Reprinted in 1973 by Greenwood Press,
a division of Williamhouse-Regency Inc.

Library of Congress Catalogue Card Number 73-10850

ISBN 0-8371-7040-0

Printed in the United States of America

PREFACE.

THIS Museum issues a series of handbooks of which this volume is the fourth dealing with primitive races. The earlier issues treat of restricted culture areas in North America, but the present volume presents the essential facts as to the racial and cultural characters of the Philippine Islands population. As will be seen in the following pages a large part of the Island population is Christian and far on the road to cultural assimilation. Neither in the Museum collections nor in this book do we attempt to describe the lives of these people, but only state their racial and historic relations to the Pagan and Mohammedan tribes still more or less successfully resisting the encroachments of European culture. As in most studies of this kind, the primitive peoples still surviving are taken as indications of what was once the prevailing culture of the whole population.

The racial exhibits in the American Museum of Natural History are grouped by halls, each hall containing collections from one geographical area. Thus one hall is devoted to the people of the Philippines and the neighboring East Indian islands. The collection in this hall furnishes illustrations of many subjects treated in this book. As a part of the wall decoration, there are many specimens of wood native to the islands, suggesting the floral and economic wealth of the country; but within the exhibition cases are objects selected to represent the skill and art of the less civilized tribes. The bulk of the collections came from the United States exhibit at the St. Louis Exposition of 1904, purchased and presented by Morris K. Jesup in 1905. To this were added later the Laura E. Benedict Bagobo collection and the Frederick Starr collections, purchased from the Jesup Fund. In addition generous donations of collections were made by William S. Kahnweiler, H. E. Bard, Charles H. Senff, and William Demuth. Dean C. Worcester presented prints from his unrivaled collection of negatives from which were taken many of the accompanying illustrations.

5

We are also indebted to the Philippine Bureau of Science for the frontispiece and Figs. 32 and 44. The maps and drawings were prepared by Mr. S. Ichikawa of the Museum staff. It may be added that the author, on leave of absence from the University of California, filled a temporary appointment in the Museum as Associate Curator in charge of the Philippine collections, during which interval this volume was written.

CONTENTS

MAPS AND ILLUSTRATIONS
MAPS

NOTE

Map 6: Peoples of the Philippines, opposite page 230,
was changed from color to black and white for the reprint edition.

FIRST EDITION, 1919
REVISED EDITION, 1928

INTRODUCTION

THERE are several things that make the peoples of the Philippines interesting.

First, is the size and position of the islands. They are the largest of the possessions of the United States; and the only one of consequence in the Eastern Hemisphere.

Then, the Filipinos form a considerable and a growing nationality. There are over ten millions of them—more than the population of the majority of European countries. The increase of numbers has been steady for several centuries, and the resources of the islands are so great that there is every reason to expect the growth to continue.

Finally, the Philippines furnish an unusual story to the student of the development of civilization. Layer after layer of culture is recognizable, giving a complete transition from the most primitive condition to full participation in Western civilization. This is a most happy circumstance for the historian, because of its rarity outside of Europe and western Asia. In aboriginal America, in most of Africa, in Australia, over large tracts of the Oceanic island world, the student of civilization finds only peoples that lack a background of history. Nation differs from nation and tribe from tribe in these regions; but it is usually difficult to be sure how any given people differs from its condition of only a few hundred years before. The investigator of these areas is therefore compelled to begin his operations almost wholly in the field of geography. It is only after he has laboriously worked out all possible classifications on the basis of locality, that he can commence to convert this knowledge into an expression of probable time sequence of development. Even then, his course must be devious and his results largely hypothetical. The problem in these parts of the world may be compared to the task of tracing the life history of an individual without direct knowledge of the events of his career, merely as a reconstruction from his condition at the present moment, his relations with other personalities, and such documents and tangible evidences as he may carry with him. Such a reconstruction is not of course impossible, but it is naturally difficult, indirect, and approximate.

In the Philippines it is true that direct historical records also go back only four hundred years. But a constellation of circumstances has brought it about that the various ancient and modern influences that have reached the islands are often traceable to their sources. The result is that whereas in Africa or native America we can almost never tell offhand whether a particular institution or name or invention is three hundred or three thousand years old, and large masses of circumstantial evidence must be analyzed before an answer to such questions may be even attempted, we can, in the Philippines, often see that one custom is very ancient and primitive, that a second must have reached the archipelago subsequently and from a foreign source, and that the third is a quite recent importation.

In other words, the stratification of civilization is much better preserved in the Philippines than in most other parts of the world which the ethnologist deals with. The task of tracing this stratification, and distinguishing through it the outlines of development, is therefore comparatively fruitful. This does not mean that obscure points are lacking and that no problems remain to be solved. But the contours of the cultural events of the last two thousand years are substantially clear. We can peel off layer after layer of civilization and come to its original kernel with some assurance of certainty and without being forced to draw too heavily on imagination.

The outer of these layers, the most continuous, and by far the most important politically and economically, may be called the Christian one. Since their conquest by Legazpi in 1564–71, the most fertile, accessible, and populous parts of the Philippines were under Spanish rule for more than three centuries. Wherever Spanish power was at all firm, the natives were promptly, and in the main thoroughly, converted to Christianity. Near the centers of population they came also to live under economic conditions approximating those of European countries. A good deal was done for education; enough, at any rate, for the first American census, made only a few years after the taking over of the islands from Spain, to show that nearly one-half of the population was in some measure literate. Certain classes had become as thoroughly cultivated, in the European sense, as Europeans. The mass of the population retained many of the older customs; but the dominant aspects of their life were western and Christian. Nearly nine-tenths of the inhabitants of the Philippines are today in this condition.

In the extreme south of the archipelago, in and about the great island of Mindanao, followers of

Mohammed had begun to establish themselves about 1380, less than two centuries before the coming of the Spaniards. Still later, they had obtained a foothold farther north in the islands, as on Mindoro, and on Manila Bay, where ruler and court were Mohammedan when the Spaniards arrived. In this district, Mohammedanism quickly yielded to Christianity without leaving a trace; but in the south it long resisted Spanish encroachment by force of arms, and even at the present day maintains its sway over several hundred thousand natives. On the side of religion, the effect of Mohammedanism on its converts has been fully as thorough as that of Christianity. The latter religion, however, was imparted by a dominant Caucasian race which continued to hold itself more or less aloof from the natives, whereas Mohammedanism was introduced by kindred East Indian immigrants who quickly amalgamated with the aborigines. Christianity and Spanish occupation also involved rather deep-going economic change. The Mohammedan contented himself with exacting such tribute as he could without radically altering existing conditions. Except therefore for a few importations, especially in the matter of weapons, he worked a less profound change in the general culture of the natives than the Christian.

Back of these two great movements of religion and general culture, lies a deeper one, the most determinative of Philippine civilization. This is an influence, or rather a set of influences, emanating from India. These influences did not bring a definitely crystallized religious cult, or if so, the cult had already disappeared before the discovery of the islands by Europeans. They did import a mass

of religious ideas, practices, and names, a considerable body of Sanskrit words, a system of writing,
the art of metal working, a vast body of mechanical
and industrial knowledge, and unquestionably a
much greater degree of cultivation and refinement
than had existed previously.

There is no reason to believe that the bulk of this
immensely valuable cultural material was brought
into the Philippines by Hindus coming directly
from India. If so, we should expect to find ruins
and other ancient remains as evidences of their
occupancy; and such have not been discovered. It
is well known that the western East Indies were
subjected to deep Hindu influences, which are estimated to have commenced about the beginning of
the Christian era. By the fifth or sixth century
much of Sumatra was Buddhist, and from the sev-
enth century on the Buddhist empire of Shri-Vijaya,
with its center near Palembang on that island, dom-
inated much of the East Indies and even parts of
Indo-China for several hundred years. As this
realm declined, its power passed to the Brahman-
istic empire of Madjapahit in Java, which endured,
with dependencies in Borneo and other islands, until
its power was broken by Mohammedans only a few
years before the discovery of America. With this
sort of interrelations going on for a millennium or
more, and one island tending to impart its acquisi-
tions to the next, it is conceivable that a large proportion of Indian culture reached the Philippines
without many or even any Hindus having set foot
upon them. It is of course also possible that expeditions led by Indian princes or adventurers now
and then established themselves on the islands and
thus aided in the more gradual diffusion that was

taking place. We know, however, that few Arabs accompanied the expeditions which first carried Mohammedanism to the Philippines. The immigrants were mainly Mohammedanized Malays from Johore and Sumatra, and, relatively to the indigenous population, few in numbers. As the Hindus are not a typically maritime nation, it is likely that the manner in which their civilization reached the Philippines was even less direct than Mohammedanism —that is, more completely dependent upon native channels of transmission.

The Indian influence, perhaps because it was older and continued longer, was more pervasive than the Mohammedan one. It was most profound, of course, along the coast and in the lowlands, but penetrated even to the mountainous interior of the larger islands. There is no tribe in the Philippines, no matter how primitive and remote, in whose culture of today elements of Indian origin cannot be traced.

Only the structure of society seems to have been affected very little. The Mohammedan brought the idea of kingship—of the sultan or *dato*—and with it that of the state. Thus it was that the Mohammedan tribes were the only ones in the Philippines who possessed any political organization, and through this organization were the only ones able to resist Spanish subjection for any considerable time. The Hindu however, though he had long been familiar with the institution of kingship, did not establish kingdoms, nor did he introduce his distinctive system of caste. His greatest contributions to the civilization of the Philippines were clearly on the side of knowledge and thought and religion, as has been characteristic of his part in the history of culture at all times.

Contemporaneous with these contacts or indirect transmissions from India, and long surviving them, was a set of relations between southern China and the Philippines. China is very much nearer than India and has enjoyed a high measure of civilization for at least as long. Probably as far back as the ninth century, and possibly within a few hundred years after the opening of the Christian era, the Chinese visited the Philippines; and from the thirteenth on, their records tell of trade and describe the habits of the natives. For many hundreds of years, pottery vessels of certain special types continued to be exported from China to the Philippines and Borneo and came to constitute the most treasured heirlooms even of interior tribes that had never set eyes on a junk. Today, the gongs which the uncivilized Filipinos use as one of their chief musical instruments, or at least their bronze, is said to come from China. Many other instances of trade relations might be cited; yet it is curious that with all this prolonged contact only material objects seem to have been carried from the more civilized to the less civilized country. There is scarcely an institution, piece of knowledge, or religious belief current in the Philippines that can be derived with certainty from China. The difference in this respect between India and China is remarkable, and illustrates significantly the distinctive tempers of these two great nationalities.

Behind and below all the foregoing is the native East Indian or Malaysian core of primitive culture with which the Filipinos must have begun their career. This kernel or substratum is preserved in its purest form among the inland mountaineers of northern Luzon, the largest island in the archipelago. This group of tribes, sometimes designated collectively under the name Igorot, were less affected than any others by Hindu influences. Mohammedanism did not reach them at all, and Christianity mainly in its economic aspects and at that chiefly at the fringes. By subtracting from their life, as it has survived to the present day, whatever can be recognized as Hindu in origin, we obtain a fairly definite picture of what the older Filipino and Malaysian culture must have been. On matching this picture with that presented by the more advanced tribes, we can recognize what is primitive among the latter; and find it to be no inconsiderable element. The constitution of society, the relations of man to man within the group, and of group to group, are still essentially of the pre-Christian and pre-Hindu type over most of the Philippines.

Here our positive knowledge ends. There should be another chapter to the story, because we know that another stratum of culture must have underlain the early Malaysian one. We know this because there are remnants of a population that is distinct from the Malaysians and must have preceded it. In several of the Philippine islands there survive some thousands of small, broad-nosed, curly-haired, black people,—Negritos, "little blacks," the Spaniards called them, and the name has remained with them. Physically, they are fundamentally of a different type from the brown, lanky-haired Malaysian whose affinities are Mongoloid. So distinctive, in fact, are the two races that it is inconceivable that they could have evolved side by side in the same region. The localization of the Negritos, and their inferiority in arts as well as numbers, are such that the first Spanish settlers were driven to the conclusion that they must represent the aboriginal inhabitants of the Philippines who had been in possession before the first members of the brown race reached the shores of the archipelago. No other view regarding them appears tenable today.

Now, the Negrito of the dim pre-Malaysian days must have had some rudiments of culture of his own, simple and savage though it undoubtedly was; and a knowledge of this would certainly be of the greatest interest. Unfortunately however he has always been so weak and backward, as compared with the overwhelming preponderance of the Malaysian, that ever since we know anything of him he has been in a position of cultural dependence and parasitism toward the brown man. He has entirely lost the distinctive language which he must once have had; and while his culture is extremely meager, practically everything in it is only a simplified imitation of what the Filipino proper possesses. It is only his racial type, his blood and physical appearance, that the Negrito has maintained; and this is usually mixed along the borders of the regions which he occupies, just as strains of Negrito blood are often recognizable among the Filipino tribes who are neighbors to him. The Negrito is so utterly different from everything else human in the islands that it will be necessary to consider him more in detail in a separate section. But unfortunately most that can be said about him from the point of view of the history of civilization is, that while he must have had a form of culture antecedent to all others that we know in the Philippines, this culture has been so worn down by thousands of years of contact with more advanced peoples, that its peculiar qualities can only be surmised.

Such, in its broad outlines and viewed retrospectively, has been the history of man and his institutions in the Philippines. In the pages that follow, the native civilization will be taken up more in detail according to its various aspects of economics, society, industry, thought, and knowledge, with an attempt to preserve under each head the guiding thread of sequence here sketched.

CHAPTER I

THE ISLANDS AND THEIR POPULATION

The Islands. The Philippines are a group of over four hundred considerable islands—plus about six thousand smaller ones—which with few exceptions are separated from one another only by narrow channels. There is probably no other archipelago in the world that contains as many islands so compactly situated. The total land area aggregates 115,000 square miles, or somewhat more than the state of Arizona and a little less than Great Britain and Ireland combined. The largest island is Luzon in the north; the next, Mindanao in the south. In a geographical sense, these two islands are the mainstay of the archipelago; they make up two-thirds of its area. Between them lies the central or Bisayan group, which consists of numerous small islands interspersed among seven of medium size: Panay, Negros, Cebu, Bohol, Leyte, Samar, and Masbate. The largest of these is about one-eighth the size of Luzon. Outside of Luzon, Mindanao, and the central group, the Philippine Islands are small, and often lie in chains which form bridges, as it were, to other parts of the East Indies.

The first of these bridges reaches northward from the northern end of Luzon, and is obviously nothing but a continuation of the main cordillera that follows the east coast of this island. This chain consists of the small Babuyanes and Batanes, which stretch in the direction of Formosa. From the farthest of the Batanes, Formosa is visible in clear weather.   This large island in turn fronts the coast of China at no great distance.

The main cordillera traverses the entire irregular length of Luzon, reappears in Samar and Leyte, and again forms a steep wall along the eastern coast of Mindanao.   Here it becomes submerged in the Pacific Ocean, although its progress can be followed in islands stretching toward Halmahera.   Another chain stretches from a parallel range of Mindanao via the Sangir Islands' to the northern arm of the great island of Celebes, whose length the range again traverses.

Another and more westerly cordillera can be traced through the greater part of Luzon.   It dips into the sea somewhat sooner than the eastern, but rises once more to form the backbone of the Island of Negros, and again the western range of Mindanao.   Here it submerges again to form the Sulu Islands, of which the chief are Basilan, Sulu or Jolo, and Tawi-Tawi.   These are not very large, but they are well known as the center of Mohammedan influence in the Philippines.   The general course of the chain of Sulu islands is southwestward, and they reach very nearly to the northeastern tip of the great island of Borneo.

Still another of the arms which the Philippines reach out toward other parts of the East Indies is formed by the islands of Mindoro and Palawan. These stretch in a southwesterly direction from central Luzon to northern Borneo.   Mindoro is very near Luzon, but the channel separating the two is fairly deep, and there is also deep water between it and Palawan.   In former geological ages Mindoro appears to have been connected alternately with Luzon and Palawan, probably last with the latter.

These facts are reflected in certain peculiarities of its animal and plant life. It is interesting that in its human history Mindoro has also always maintained a certain aloofness.

Palawan or Paragua, although very narrow, extends some 250 miles, and is the third longest island in the Philippines. The history of its human occupation is similar to that of Mindoro. Palawan is separated from Borneo by only slight depths of sea, and geographically forms nothing but an outlying extension of this island with which its flora and fauna are definitely connected.

Continental Affiliations. The East Indies are divided by geologists and biologists into two major areas and a smaller intermediate tract. The western area constitutes a partly submerged portion of the continent of Asia. The eastern area is similarly linked with Australia. In each case there is a great shelf, submarine but covered by only a shallow layer of ocean, extending out from the mass of the continent. The Asiatic or Sunda shelf carries the islands of Sumatra, Java, and Borneo. The Australian or Sahul shelf carries New Guinea. So shallow are these shelves that a rise of the sea bottom by 150 feet would unite Sumatra, Java, and Borneo with Asia, and a rise of only 65 feet, New Guinea with Australia. In past geological periods such slight elevations have repeatedly occurred, or the sea level has been sufficiently lower to establish the connections. The result is that the animals and plants of the western East Indies are essentially Asiatic; those of New Guinea, Australian. In Sumatra and Borneo occur such forms as the elephant, rhinoceros, tapir, tiger, and orang-utan, characteristic of Asia. Australia specializes in kangaroos and other marsupial mammals, in eucalyptus trees, and, in New Guinea, in birds of paradise. Not since the Cretaceous age has there been land connection between Asia and Australia. The periods of the Tertiary and Quaternary that have elapsed since then account for the deep differences in the animal and plant life of the two areas. Both continents have been unusually stable for a long time past—probably since their separation—at least in the parts turned toward each other. To be sure, dry land has become archipelago and vice versa; but while such changes may loom large on the map, the alterations of level have been so slight as to be insignificant from the point of view of geological structure.

Between the two continental areas, however, lies a region which to the geologist represents an antithesis; an area of deep sea basins and troughs with bordering ridges, some of which rise above the ocean as islands; an area also of unusual instability—blocks of it rising and falling. This area is the one that includes the Philippines, Celebes, probably the Moluccas, Timor, and smaller islands. Parts of this area may at one time or another have been in contact with the Asiatic and Australian continental masses, or have received animal and plant forms from them. At any rate, the fauna and flora are neither typically Asiatic nor Australian, but transitional. Philippine life contains a rather larger Asiatic element—of west Malaysian form—than it contains Australian or New Guinean elements. But all the great mammals of Borneo and Sumatra are lacking; and it is clear that the archipelago is part of the transition area.

Two famous "biological lines," Wallace's and

Weber's, are interpretable as essentially the western and eastern edges of the unstable transition area—or to put it the other way round, as the southeastern limit of the Asiatic mass and northwestern limit of the Australian mass where these abut on the intermediate region.

Racially and historically, that is in regard to man, distributions tend to follow the same areas and lines. The islands that belong geologically to Asia, and those of the intermediate area, are inhabited by a brown, straight-haired people, the so-called "Malayan" race of the older books, whose relationship is primarily Mongoloid and therefore Asiatic. East of Weber's line, that is, in the islands associated with Australia, a black, broad-nosed, curly-haired people prevails far out into the Pacific, but not on the islands most remote from Australia. These are the Papuans of New Guinea and the Melanesians or "black islanders." The main land-mass of Australia was held by a somewhat different, wavy-haired people, who were however also black and broad-nosed. The Australians are at least superficially like Negroes; the Papuans and Melanesians are reckoned as belonging outright to the Negroid family. The racial contrast is therefore as sharp as the geological one and conforms to it.

Even religion and type of customs have tended to coincide rather closely with the geological line of division. Mohammedanism has spread about as far eastward as the brown peoples, but has been most deeply implanted in the islands of the Asiatic continental shelf. At an earlier period, Hinduism penetrated to about an equal distance. Yet the islands in which the influence of India was really powerful, as attested by the ruins in Hindu style of architec-

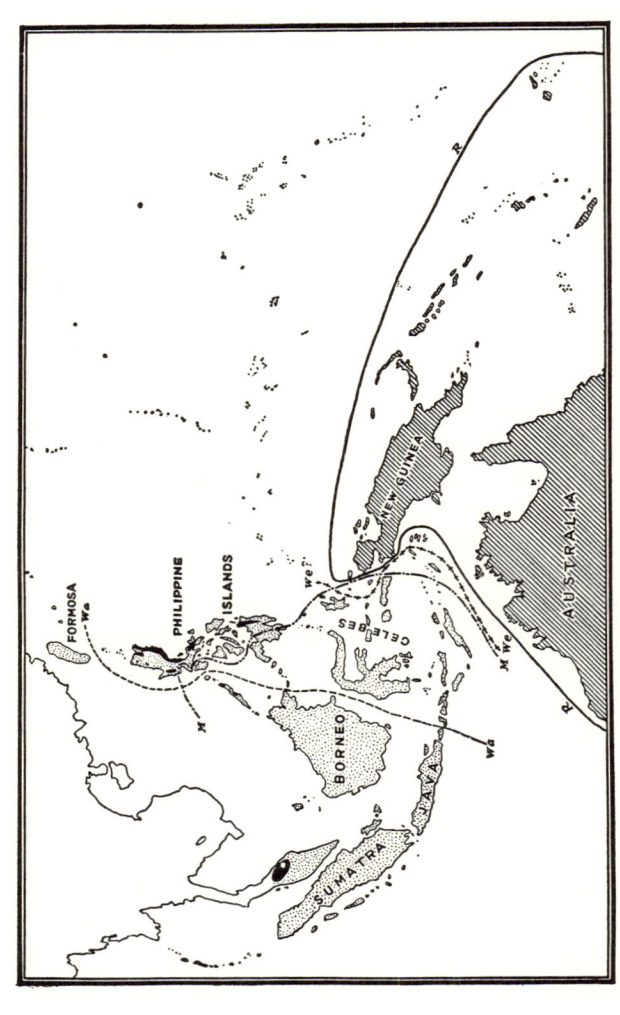

Map 1. RACES AND NATURAL AREAS

Black: Negritos. *Hatching:* Other black peoples: Papuans, Melanesians, Australians. *Stippling:* Brown peoples: Malayans, Indonesians, Micronesians, Polynesians.

Continuous line: R, Demarcation between black and brown races.

Broken lines: Wa, Wallace's line, as modified by recent studies, eastern limit of Asiatic continental shelf: We, Weber's line, similarly modified, western limit of Australian continental shelf. Between lies a geologically unstable area, with flora and fauna transitional between those of the Asiatic and Australian areas.

Dotted line: M, eastern limit of Mohammedanism. The close correspondence of this with Weber's line is notable.

26

ture and sculpture, are precisely those which belong with Asia: namely, Sumatra, Borneo, Java. The Philippines, Celebes, and the other islands of the geologically unstable intermediate zone contain no such remains. In short, Wallace's line, as now generally accepted in modified form, pretty well marks the limit of effectively prevalent Hinduism and Mohammedanism, just as Weber's line, also as now modified, nearly coincides with the outer limit of Hindu and Mohammedan influence as well as the primary race separation. It is not often that geological, biological, and human history coincide so closely in their respective cleavages.

Topography and Climate. The larger Philippine islands, especially Luzon and Mindanao, contain considerable areas of lowland swamp and lakes. The general character of the archipelago, however, like that of the other East Indies, is mountainous. In fact, it is quite remarkable, in all this part of the world, to what an altitude the mountains rise, compared with the size of the land masses. The highest peaks in the Philippines fall somewhat short of the greatest elevations reached in some other groups, but the altitudes of about eight thousand feet attained by Mounts Mayon in Luzon, Kanlaon in Negros, and Halcon in Mindoro, and of nearly ten thousand feet by Apo in Mindanao, and Pulog in Luzon, are by no means insignificant. The country in general, therefore, is distinctly rugged, and the dominant feature of the geography is the juxtaposition of the sea and of steep ranges and high peaks with only a narrow belt of rich alluvial coast intervening.

It is this lowland region that has always held the bulk of the population. Two-thirds of the modern

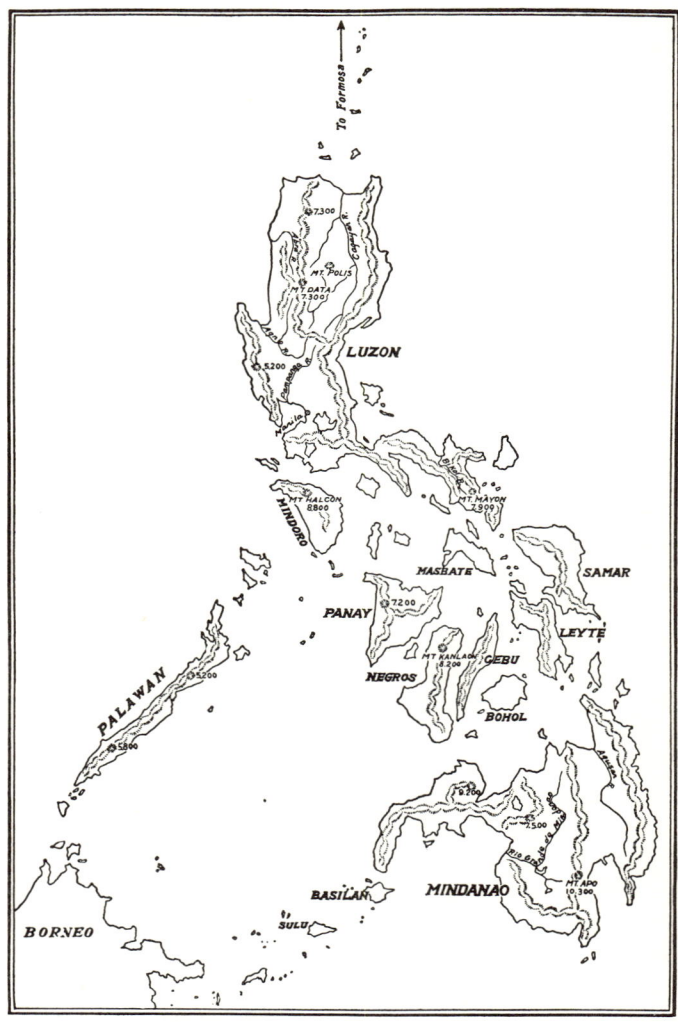

Map 2. PRINCIPAL ISLANDS, RIVERS, RANGES, AND PEAKS
OF THE PHILIPPINES

inhabitants live on the coast, one-third in the interior. With an estimated eleven thousand miles of shore line in the archipelago, this proportion seems only natural.

Many of the peaks are volcanic, usually quiescent, but twelve of them permanently or intermittently active. There have been a number of disastrous eruptions within the historic period and no doubt many others in prehistoric times. So far as known, the effects of these outbursts have however always been local, and while they have caused considerable loss of life and property in the districts immediately affected, the islands as a whole, and the course of human history on them, seem not to have been seriously disturbed by these cataclysms. The same may be said of the earthquakes which are both frequent and violent in most of the Philippines. The city of Manila has several times suffered severely; but the natives, before their Christianization, building their houses wholly of wood or bamboo and maintaining no public works, have never endured more than passing inconveniences. The typhoons which visit the northern and central islands probably caused much more destruction.

The Philippines reach from the fifth degree of north latitude to the nineteenth. They therefore lie wholly within the tropics, although the Batanes group, north of Luzon, stretches to within little more than a hundred miles of the limits of this zone. The temperature, as might be expected in an island climate, is remarkably equable. The warmest and coldest months in Manila differ by less than four degrees Centigrade, and the difference between the annual average temperatures in the northern and southern parts of the islands is only about one degree Centigrade. The climate, with the exception of a few localities, is an unusually healthy one for the tropics. The rainfall is very variable, as might be expected from the irregular configuration of land and sea and the interspersed character of the mountain ranges. It is however generally fairly heavy, ranging from forty to one hundred and eighty inches a year,—the observed average for the whole archipelago is ninety-three inches,—or from two to four times as much as in most parts of the temperate zone. Even those districts in the interior of northern Luzon which are sometimes spoken of as semi-arid, must be understood as being so only in a comparative sense; they probably receive more rain than most parts of the United States. The precipitation is, on the whole, seasonal, but the seasons vary as much as the amount of rainfall. On some islands one side is in the dry period while the other is in the wet. The western flank of the archipelago north of Mindanao has a wet summer and dry winter. The eastern flank, from central Luzon south, has no dry season, but the rainfall reaches a pronounced maximum in winter. The remainder of the archipelago is divided between two intermediate types of climate.

The combination of continuous tropical warmth and great precipitation produces the usual result: a rapid growth of a heavy and luxuriant vegetation. Practically the whole surface of the Philippines was naturally clothed with dense forest: the regions— like parts of northern Luzon—which are now more or less denuded, appearing to be so through human agencies. Over most of the islands, in fact, man is forced to maintain a constant struggle against the powerful growth impulse of the vegetation,

which threatens everywhere to choke out his means
of existence or reduce him to a parasitic condition.
Hardly is a patch cleared for agriculture when the
jungle or rank growths of tough coarse grass invade
it.   The second year's crop is almost invariably inferior to the first, and it is only in the minority of
instances that a field can be cultivated with profit a
fourth or fifth time.   With more labor in checking
the wild vegetation than the produce is worth, the
only recourse is to start fresh, and this the native
has done from time immemorial.   He burns off and
clears another few acres of the forest, only to
abandon this after a few seasons.   This is the well-
known *kaingin* system, which has been enormously
destructive of valuable timber, but is the only feasible method of working the soil under primitive and
semi-civilized conditions and without irrigation.

Population.   The fertility of the islands is so
great that they are capable of supporting an enormous population, and, relatively to many other
parts of the world, they have apparently done so
for a long time past.   The number of inhabitants
in the archipelago at the time of the Spanish discovery and conquest in the sixteenth century is put
by some students at half a million, by others at
somewhat more.   These are small figures as compared with the nine to ten millions that at present
find easy subsistence; but they are large numbers
for a people that could at most be said to have attained barely to semi-civilization.   If we accept the
population of the archipelago at the time of discovery as approximately two-thirds of a million, it
contained about as many souls as then lived in what
is now the United States in an area twenty-five or
thirty times as great.   Even at the lowest computa-

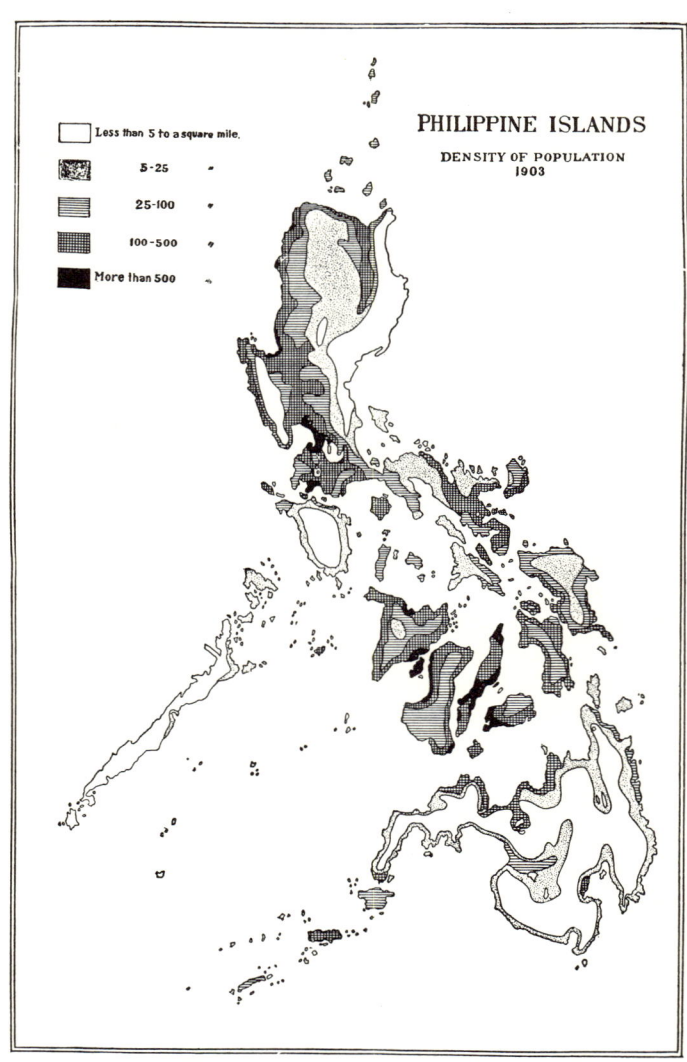

PHILIPPINE ISLANDS

DENSITY OF POPULATION
1903

Less than 5 to a square mile.

5 - 25   "

25-100   "

100-500   "

More than 500   "

Map 3.   DENSITY OF POPULATION IN 1903

The population in 1916 was estimated to be one-fourth greater than was assumed for the preparation of this map, but the principal change made would be the designation of certain areas in the interior of northern Luzon one or two shades darker.   The United States as a whole would barely fall into the class here shown by the middle of the five shades used.

tion, five inhabitants per square mile must be allowed the Philippines in the pre-European period. This is a higher figure than prevailed in any regions of the aboriginal New World other than certain parts of Mexico and Peru.

An acre of rice grown under irrigation or in swampy land supports from three to five persons, or very nearly an average household in Java, in the Christianized portions of the Philippines, and among the primitive mountaineers of Luzon. As the labor required to farm such a tract is in most cases rather moderate and leaves certain seasons of the year entirely free, it is clear both how a considerable condensation of population could have taken place in prehistoric times, and why the population has tended to increase steadily at a considerable rate ever since. In 1591 Spanish tribute lists indicated a population, at the estimated ratio of four souls to one tribute, of 667,000. This figure excludes all the unsubjected mountain tribes and all the Mohammedans; in fact, almost the whole of the island of Mindanao. For two centuries increase continued, though rather slowly. In 1800 there were about a million and a half Christians in the archipelago. By 1840 this number had doubled, and by 1887 had doubled again, to six millions. The American census of 1903 showed nearly seven million Christians, and the latest estimate, for 1916, reckons 8,400,000; to whom more than a million Pagans, Mohammedans, and foreigners must be added. The present rate of increase is at least one and one-half percent annually, and unless adversely affected by social causes which have not yet developed, the native population should attain twenty millions within forty years. In fact, it does not seem inconceivable that within a century the population might reach fifty or even a hundred millions.

This may appear an extravagant estimate; but it must be remembered that Java, an island not much larger than Luzon alone, now contains thirty million souls, or fifteen times as many as a hundred and forty years ago. Only a tenth of the area of the Philippines is at present under cultivation. The subprovince of Ifugao, inhabited by the distinctly primitive tribe of the same name, is computed to contain 132,000 inhabitants with a total plane area of perhaps 750 square miles. The district is extremely rugged, and less than fifty square miles of it are actually cultivated, the lesser half of these being in rice. This means that more than two thousand people working with primitive tools derive their subsistence from each square mile cultivated. These truly astonishing conditions need only be appreciated to make almost any prophecy of the future populousness of the Philippines seem justifiable.

With these half-tamed, head-hunting Ifugao living more than 170 to the square mile in their mountains, it is not surprising that certain of the civilized districts show an enormous congestion, far greater, in fact, than any parts of Europe but those industrially most active. Northern, central, and southern Luzon, as well as at least four of the central islands, contain tracts that sustain more than five hundred persons to the mile. In 1820, the ratio for the United States was five. The only portions of the Philippines that fall below this figure today are certain areas in the interior of Mindanao and two wild mountain ranges in Luzon. Even Mindoro and Palawan, the most sparsely settled islands, contain populations of thirteen and eight to the mile when considered as a whole, or more than many of our western states; while Luzon, with an area equal to that of Pennsylvania, but without immigration, manufactures, or industries other than agriculture, supports half as many inhabitants.

It cannot be assumed, because the population to-day, after more than three centuries of Spanish rule, has become so dense, that it would have arrived at the same high total had the natives been left to themselves. But it is interesting that what the Spaniard accomplished was to do away with the social causes that had been restraining the natural impulse to increase which had long been latent in the Filipino. He did not increase his power of drawing subsistence from the soil. He introduced order, limited piracy, abolished human sacrifice, suppressed war, head-hunting, all the endless feuds that not only claimed thousands annually but destroyed homes and plantations and rendered life forever unsettled. As soon as these checks began to be removed, the population increased of itself; once they were definitely eliminated, it grew fast and steadily. New land of course was reclaimed, and where conditions permitted, as in the irrigated districts, kept under permanent cultivation.

But the available soil was utilized only in small part after all, and its yield per acre or mile remained nearly constant. The plow was introduced, and the buffalo yoked to it, where wooden spades and the hands had sufficed before. This change reduced the labor which the Filipino spent on his subsistence; it did not greatly increase his food supply. Had the Filipino been able to devise an efficient political organization and stable government for himself, there is no doubt that his economic mechanisms, combined with the fertility of his country, would have enabled him to become, even in the pre-European period, several times more populous than he was at his discovery.

Black Peoples: The Negritos. The Negrito, the earliest inhabitant of the Philippines, is a most peculiar type of humanity. He is black in the sense in which the African Negro is black, and his hair is thick, short, and woolly. He can and often does grow a full beard, and his trunk bears a perceptible coating of body hair. His jaws protrude, but the face tapers to a narrow chin. His head is well rounded, its width averaging almost exactly five-sixths of the length. The nose is extremely broad: there are about as many individuals in which the transverse diameter of this organ exceeds its greatest length, as the reverse. This is of course a Negroid trait.

But the most marked characteristic of the Negrito, that which has earned him his name and suffices to set him off sharply from all true Negroes, is his diminutive stature. He is truly a pygmy, with an average height equivalent to that of a thirteen year old American boy. Nearly every group that has been measured shows a stature of appreciably less than 150 cm., or five feet. The women, of course, are proportionally shorter. The single known group of Negrito affinity which runs a few inches taller, the Mamanua of Mindanao, may be assumed to have acquired its increased stature through intermixture with Malaysian neighbors. At the same time, the Negrito is in no sense a dwarf, nor does he ordinarily make the impression of being an essentially underfed and stunted variety of man. The head is not disproportionately large, and the

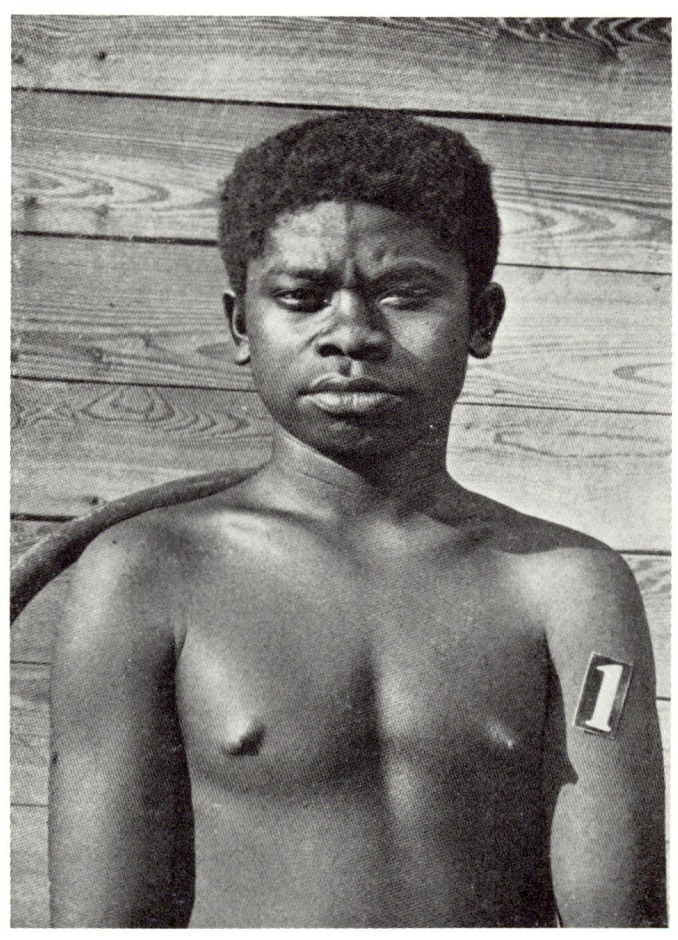

Fig. 1. NEGRITO MAN

Fig. 2. NEGRITO GIRL

body in general is neatly and cleanly symmetrical.

We have then before us a thoroughly separate and apparently ancient type of man which cannot possibly be regarded as a variety or modification of the race that constitutes the bulk of Philippine population.

The Negrito lives in scattered bands in a variety of localities, but always in the forested mountains. Four or five of these regions are in Luzon, one in Mindanao, and one in Palawan. These groups often bear diverse appellations: thus the two last-mentioned are known as Mamanua and Batak, respectively. The name Aeta has often been applied to the Negritos as a whole; it is the designation given the race in the language of the Tagalog; but the Tagalog were acquainted with only a small proportion of the stock.

The number of undoubted Negritos in the Philippines is probably between thirty and forty thousand. They constitute a small fraction of one percent of the total population of the islands. There are more Chinese immigrants than survivors of this, the most primitive of the native races.

The generally accepted theory that the Negrito originally held all or most of the Philippines, is borne out by the fact that at the time of discovery he was more widely diffused than at present. The Bisayan island of Negros derives its name from having harbored a distinctly black people, who can scarcely have been anything but Negritos. In its interior, as well as in the central mountains of the two other large Bisayan islands of Panay and Samar, there live today uncivilized people who have sometimes been described as Negritos, while other observers have classified them as rude Malaysians.

The islands of Gimaras off Panay, and Polillo to the east of Luzon, also contain people in whom a distinct Negrito strain is probable. There are moreover groups in southern Luzon that may or may not contain a Negrito element. Most of these little peoples of doubtful or partial Negrito affinities were classified in the first American census as "Bukidnon," an apt native term meaning Hill people. The name is however unfortunate in omitting all reference to their supposed physical type; and doubly so, because Bukidnon has now become the official and accepted designation of an important pagan tribe in Mindanao which is entirely free of any suspicion of containing Negrito elements. The scattered half Negrito or doubtful Negrito groups are therefore best brought together under their Spanish appellations of Remontados or Monteses, in English, "Hill Men." While it is important to recognize that they are quite clearly not a unit, there is little doubt that at least some of their bands contain a decided Negrito element, and in a few it may preponderate. The aggregate number of these Hill people is perhaps somewhat greater than that of the pure Negrito, but probably falls short of fifty thousand.

There are three other parts of the East Indies in which the presence of Negritos has been definitely confirmed. One of these is in the interior of the Malay Peninsula, where the Semang are of this type; another group comprises the inhabitants of the Andaman Islands in the Indian Ocean north of Sumatra; the third includes a series of scarcely explored tribes in New Guinea. These groups agree with the Philippine Negritos in being excessively short, black-skinned, frizzly-haired, medium to round-headed, and broad-nosed.

It is rather difficult to understand the distribution of the Negritos in four such scattered spots as the Philippines, New Guinea, the Malay Peninsula, and the Andaman Islands. The question naturally arises how it is that if they once occupied the intervening and surrounding islands and have been submerged by the subsequent Malaysians without leaving a trace, they have been able to maintain themselves in substantial purity of type in these four regions alone.

It is also certain that there is a close similarity of physical type between the East Indian Negritos and the Negrillos or pygmy blacks of Central Africa. Most students are inclined to identify these two far-flung groups as members of the same race. This of course makes the question of their origin and dispersion still more mysterious. Several theories have been propounded in explanation, but since not one of these can muster any direct evidence in its support, it would hardly be profitable to discuss them here.

We should probably feel much more certain of understanding the Negrito problem if there were a common Negrito language; but, with one exception, no trace of such a peculiar speech has been discovered. The African pygmies speak dialects of the Bantu tongue which prevails among their full-sized neighbors. The Semang speech is interpreted as a borrowed ''Austro-Asiatic'' language. All the search that has been made in the Philippines has failed to reveal any peculiar Negrito language, or even any positive element that might be construed as a remnant of a former distinctive speech. The Philippine Negrito speaks Filipino: in fact that particular variety of Philippine speech that happens to prevail among the brown men of his district. Wherever his language has been recorded, it is nothing but a local patois of Tagalog, Cagayan, Sambal, Bikol, or whatever the Christian or pagan Malaysian of the region may talk. It is extremely likely that this was not always the case and that the language of his own which the Negrito must have possessed when he was the sole or principal owner of the islands has only gradually gone out of use, owing to his insignificant numbers as compared with the Malaysian, and because of the cultural dependence in which he has always stood toward the latter.

The Andamanese speak a peculiar language which it has not yet been possible to connect with any other variety of human speech. This they seem to have preserved only because the remoteness and small size of their islands drew no immigrants and preserved them from foreign contacts.

Negrito Life. The culture of the Negritos seems to lack specific traits. It is extremely meager, and they seem to possess no tool nor custom which was not known also to their Filipino neighbors and which they could not have derived from them. They live an unsettled existence, supporting themselves largely, and in some districts wholly, by hunting and gathering wild foods, especially roots, tubers, and honey. Externally, their mode of life is thus quite different from that of the brown Filipino; but as soon as their poor little stock of civilization is analyzed, it becomes revealed as a pale and abbreviated copy of the latter. In addition, the Negrito, with all his shyness, is wont to trade more or less with his neighbors, exchanging forest products such as rattan and beeswax for cloth, knives, iron, and ornaments.   The most useful of his possessions are therefore not even of his own manufacture.   All this renders it justifiable to consider Negrito culture as it survives today as in no sense representative of a very old and primitive culture, but as being essentially parasitic.

The relation of the black and brown men in the Philippines is well illustrated by a passage written by Father Domingo Perez in 1680.   Speaking of the customs of the Sambal, a Malaysian people now Christians, he describes how murders were compounded by payments.   If the slayer had nothing "with which to redeem the murder that he committed, he goes to the mountain and deceives some black, or steals him and drags him to his rancheria, and delivers him to the relatives of the murdered man so that they may slay the said black.   There is [no] great difficulty in this, for in mountains there they have many acquaintances among the blacks. Those blacks are not without their enemies in some rancherias of the blacks themselves, where they go to make the seizure.   And since the blacks are very revengeful in taking vengeance on their enemies, they aid the Zambals to capture them.   The Zambal gives the black, whose service he has used for that purpose, some arrows or machetes."

The house which is most frequently encountered among the Negrito is a rude lean-to of palm or banana leaves fastened to a frame that rests on a pole laid on two forked sticks some four or five feet high.   This is little more than a windbreak made to overhang sufficiently to shed the rain.   Four or five people can get some protection from the weather underneath.   A little structure of this kind is of course put up in a few minutes, and agrees well with the necessities of a more or less wandering life. In other parts, the Negritos build houses of the usual Filipino type, namely, structures with a thatched roof and a floor raised above the ground on posts, although these buildings are usually smaller and more poorly made than among the Filipinos. A Chinese account of the thirteenth century quite unmistakably tells of the Negrito living in nests high in the branches of trees. The tree house is however of general distribution among the wilder tribes of the Philippines, so that again there is nothing distinctive of the Negrito in this practice.

In a number of localities, the Negrito has taken to farming, though never on an intensive scale and usually with little care for the growth of rice, the food crop which is universally most esteemed in the Philippines and requires the most attention and skill to succeed with.

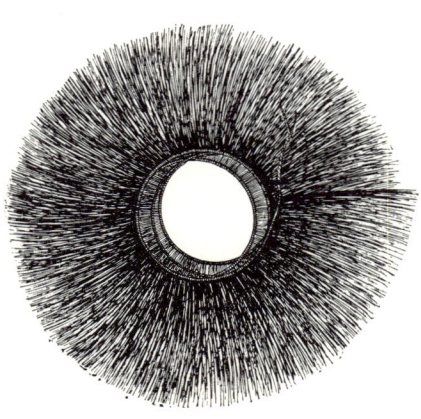

Fig. 3.   Leg Ornament of Boar's Bristles.
Negrito of Zambales

His person he decorates in some cases by sharpening his teeth to points. This is also a widespread Filipino practice. As the tattooing which the brown-skinned Filipino uses for ornament would not show on his dark skin, he decorates himself by scarifying his trunk or limbs so as to produce a series of welts. Girdles, necklaces, and neckbands of braided rattan, boar bristles, and the like, are frequently worn; but clothing is scarcely a factor wherever the Negrito is left to sole intercourse with his own kind. Sometimes he wears a clout. The women cover themselves with a little skirt of beaten bark fiber, when they cannot obtain cloth in trade.

The bow has sometimes been spoken of as the most prized possession of the Negrito and the weapon which is distinctive of him. This is only relatively true. The bow was in common use throughout the Philippines at the time of discovery, as the Spanish conquerors testified from wounds received. It has more and more gone out of use, but is still known in Luzon as well as Mindanao. It is true that the Negrito employs the weapon more than any Filipino people, but this is probably only the result of his being in the same condition in which they lived centuries ago when they could obtain but little iron for other weapons.

The Batak of Palawan are skilful in the use of a blowgun with poisoned darts, but this instrument is also known to a number of non-Negrito groups in the Philippines.

Baskets are made in much the same style and patterns as by the Filipinos, but pottery is rarely or never manufactured. It would be of little service to a people of such unsteady habits and flimsy habitations. Food is cooked either directly on the coals or in joints of bamboo whenever iron or earthenware vessels are not obtained in trade.

The musical instruments of the Negrito are more developed than might be expected from a people leading so rude a life. At least some of them are imitations of Filipino instruments. There is a simple flute, a little Jew's harp of a sliver of slit bamboo, occasionally a traded bronze gong, a guitar, and even a rude violin of bamboo.

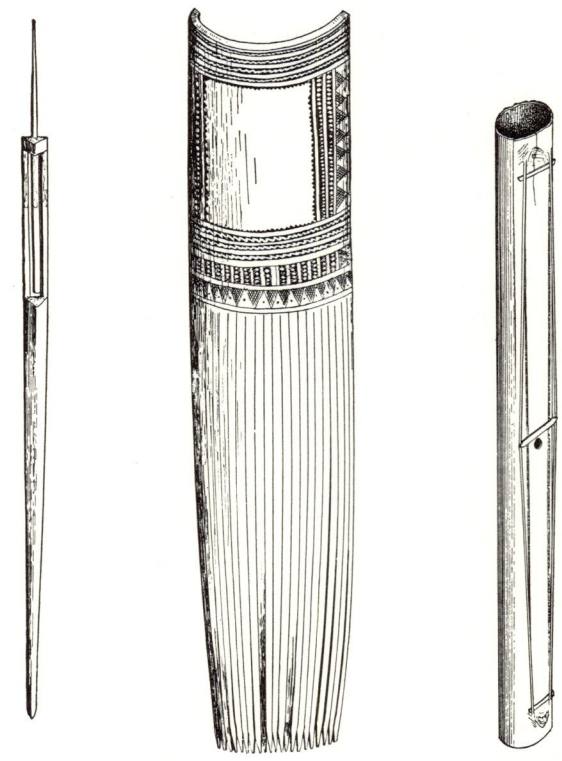

Fig. 4.   Fig. 5.

Fig. 4.   Jew's Harp and Comb worn as Hair Ornament.   Negrito.
Fig. 5.   Guitar of Bamboo, with Strings Slit Loose.   Negrito.

Negrito society and religion are very little known, but the available data again present the phenomenon of a simplified replica of Filipino institutions. For instance, marriage is by purchase of the bride, often by betrothal in youth; there is a marriage feast, the central act of the wedding being a ceremony of the bride and groom feeding each other. Slavery is known and may occasionally be practised. This is evident from the Zambales Negrito having a word denoting the condition, *alipun*. On religion even less can be said, except that its practice and that of medicine seem to be in the hands of such individuals, perhaps in the main old women, as have the power of becoming possessed by spirits.

Brown Peoples. Apart from the Negritos all the peoples of the Philippines seem at first sight to be similar in their bodily type. They are a brown-skinned, straight-haired race with scant beards and smooth skins, somewhat under the average of human height, and with distinctly slender and graceful frames moulded about delicate bones, presenting nothing at all suggestive of Negroid traits and about as little of anything Caucasian. They have usually been reckoned, together with the other inhabitants of the East Indies, as a branch of the third great division of mankind, the yellow or Mongoloid race. This does not mean that they are to be identified with the people whom we are unconsciously wont to recognize as most representative of the Mongoloids, namely, the Chinese. The Chinese are Mongolians in the narrow sense, as contrasted with the Mongoloids who embrace all the nations of Eastern Asia and aboriginal America and many of those of Oceania. In fact, there can be little doubt that the Chinese are a particular specialization of the generalized Mongoloid stem, as indeed might be expected from a people so great and so long civilized. Thus, the slant or Mongolian eye is characteristic of them and some of their nearer neighbors; but the absence of this particular

Fig. 6. Bagobo Man with Bead-Embroidered Jacket. The ear is perforated for an ornamental plug.

feature among most of the American Indians and Oceanic peoples, is no bar to the classification of these people as Mongoloids on a basis of more numerous other traits.

Indonesians and Malayans. Closer examination, however, reveals that two varieties of the Oceanic Mongoloid sub-race prevail in many parts of the East Indies. This is true in Java, in Borneo, and elsewhere, including the Philippines. The more numerous sub-type, which we may name the Malayan proper, or Deutero-Malayan, answers the description already given. It need only be added that this type is round-headed and has a nose of medium breadth.

The less numerous Indonesian [1] or Proto-Malayan sub-type differs in several respects. It averages several centimeters less in bodily height. The head is perceptibly narrower, the nose much broader. The figure is stockier, the legs are short and sturdy, and there is a general lack of the racial refinement that distinguishes the bodily contours of the proper Malayan.

In other features there is not yet known to be any difference between the two types, but those enumerated suffice to establish them as separate, although there is every indication that they are rather closely related.

In the Philippines, nine-tenths or more of the population are of the Malayan sub-type. This comprises practically all of the Christian tribes, certainly the majority of the Mohammedans, and at least some of the pagans, such as the Subanun of Mindanao. The Indonesian sub-type occurs chiefly among the pagans, and has been definitely proved

---

[1] With reference to speech, ''Indonesian'' denotes the Malaysian languages generally, irrespective of racial type—see p. 75. Proto-Malayan would be the better term except that it implies a history of race relations in the area, and this history, though probable, is only hypothetical.

Fig. 7. Bisaya Girl: Malayan Type.

Fig. 8. Tagalog: Malayan Type.

51

only for the interior of northern Luzon and the interior of Mindanao, although smaller bodies of people on other islands may yet be found to belong to this type when measurements of them shall have been made. This Indonesian type is most pronounced among the Luzon group. In Mindanao it

Fig. 9.   Fig. 10.
Figs. 9, 10.   Indonesians : Nabaloi Woman ; Bontok Man equipped for War.

is somewhat more variable. It is probable that in this island there has been some blending of the Malayan and Indonesian varieties, since some of the Mohammedan coast tribes depart from the pure Malayan type as it is found among the Christians, whereas certain of the pagans tend to resemble the Malayans.

The following figures characterize a number of tribes of the two types.

A. Mongoloid Race—Malayan (Deutero-Malayan) Variety

	Stature	Head Form	Shape of Nose
Christian Peoples:			
Cagayan	164	81	81
Ilokano	160	85	73
Pangasinan	163	84	73
Sambal	161	83	80
Pampanga	162	81	76
Tagalog of Bulacan	160	85	82
Tagalog of Rizal	158	81	80
Tagalog of Laguna	160	83	82
Tagalog of Cavite	159	83	78
Bikol	158	82	81
Bisaya of Panay	159	83	84
Bisaya of Negros	160	85	81
Bisaya of Cebu	160	84	80
Bisaya of Leyte	158	85	79
Bisaya of Samar	156	85	82
Mohammedan Peoples:			
Moro of Davao	157	82	85
Moro of Cotabato	160	81	82
Moro of Zamboanga	161	81	81
Moro of Sulu	160	83	83
Pagan Peoples:			
Valley Tinggian of Luzon	157	83	77
Mountain Tinggian of Luzon	157	80	78
Subanun of Mindanao	161	83	75
Tagakaolo of Mindanao	159	81	85

B. Mongoloid Race—Indonesian (Proto-Malayan) Variety

Pagan Peoples:			
Bontok of Luzon	155	78	100
Kankanai of Luzon	151	82	89
Nabaloi of Luzon	154	80	95
Ifugao of Luzon	155	77	102
Ilongot of Luzon	156	82	89
Manobo of Mindanao	152	82	93
Bilaan of Mindanao	155	80	(90)
Tagbanua of Palawan	155	81	93

C. NEGRITO

	Stature	Head Form	Shape of Nose
Aeta of Zambales	146	82	106
Aeta of Bataan	148	85	95
Batak of Palawan	150	81	97
Mamanua of Mindanao	[159]	84	103

SUMMARY

Range of above groups:

Malayan	157–164	80–85	73–85
Indonesian	151–156	77–82	89–102
Negrito	146–150	81–85	95–106

The origin of these two varieties of the same race of man side by side within the Philippines is best explained by the assumption of two separate waves or periods of immigration, the Indonesians arriving first and depriving the aboriginal Negritos of most of their territory, at least in the coast and lowland districts, but being in turn crowded back into the hills when the later Malayans arrived. The Malayans may or may not have come in superior numbers. It is not necessary to assume that they did. Arriving with a higher civilization perhaps already embodying many cultural elements derived from India, and possessing a more compact organization and superior weapons, they would easily have been able to establish themselves even without a preponderance of numbers. Occupying the most fertile tracts, they would tend to increase more rapidly. The Spanish occupation must also have tended strongly to accentuate the disproportion of numbers; since the inlanders were left almost wholly to their interminable blood feuds, whereas the pacified and economically advantaged Malayan tribes would multiply at a faster rate.

That something of this sort has occurred in the Philippines is probable not only on internal evidence, but because analogous conditions prevail over much of the East Indies. In Borneo, Java, Sumatra, two similar sub-types are found associated, usually in the same relation: the longer-headed and broader-nosed people mainly in the interior, the rounder-headed and narrower-nosed people along the coasts.[1] If the two types were distinct only in the Philippines, it might be imagined that they were nothing but local modifications of a single race that had reached the archipelago in one movement, but had become diversified through the respective influences of mountain and lowland habitat, with the attendant differences in mode of life. The occurrence of both types in the other islands, however, makes this explanation much less plausible than the one which assumes the successive diffusion of two separate types over the entire region.

It has been suggested that the Indonesian may be nothing but a blend of Negrito and Malayan. The shorter stature of the Indonesian and his very broad nose might at first seem to support such a view. On the other hand, the Indonesian is a distinctly straight-haired race, whereas Negrito and Negroid blood, wherever it can possibly be traced, always renders the hair at least wavy, if not curly. Furthermore, both the Malayan and the Negrito happen to coincide in being round-headed, whereas the head form of the Indonesian is distinctly longer. It is hardly possible to believe that two round-headed races should produce a long-headed blend. The distinctness of the Malayan and Indonesian

[1] In the interior of Celebes and the Malay Peninsula there occurs another short-statured and broad-nosed type, but this is wavy-haired, and appears to be of ''Veddoid'' or ''Indo-Australoid'' race rather than ''Indonesian.''

types may therefore be accepted. The Malayan is certainly Mongoloid; in many respects, his type stands very close to that which prevails in the more civilized portions of Indo-China, as in Siam. The oblique Mongoloid eye is sometimes marked in Java, and occurs occasionally among the Malayan strata in the Philippines. Inasmuch as only some five percent of the Christian Filipinos are computed to contain a strain of Chinese blood derived from Chinese immigrants, and since in certain districts— Ilokano, Tinggian, Apayao—some degree of slant eye is displayed in a larger proportion of the population, it is possible that this feature must be recognized as due to a tendency of some strength, though by no means a universal one, inhering in the Malayan variety.

The Indonesians are less distinctively Mongoloid. The slant eye is at least very rare among them, perhaps wholly absent. Their broad noses are also scarcely paralleled among other Mongoloids. It has been suggested that they are Caucasian, or of Caucasian affinities; but if this is so, the affinity must be very remote. Their lanky hair is alone sufficient to throw strong doubts on any such theory. Furthermore, their broad noses are even more un-Caucasian than un-Mongoloid; for, whereas the Mongoloid in general is medium-nosed, the Caucasian is distinctively narrow-nosed. There is also nothing specifically Negroid in the Indonesian, since his nose in spite of its breadth lacks the characteristic flat shape of the Negro organ. A connection with an Australian type has been thought of; but here also there is little if anything positive in favor of such a view.

On the whole, then, the status of the Indonesian

sub-race or variety is best summed up by its recognition as a Mongoloid type presenting fewer specific Mongoloid features than the Malayan type. On the hypothesis that the Indonesian was the earlier and the Malayan the later comer of the two sets of brown peoples, this relation is very much what might be expected.

As to the regions in which these two types originated and took their present form, and the period at which they began to swarm out from these ancestral homes, nothing is known. Even conjecture would be idle except for the supposition, which follows rather obviously from their general geographic position, that they are both likely to have had their ultimate source in southeastern Asia.

The Principal Nationalities: Christian. The local diversity of the Filipinos among themselves is rather remarkable, and argues that the past history of most groups has consisted of a long-continued occupation of the same region under conditions of limited intercourse with the outside world, broken now and then by spasmodic movements. Thirty or forty nationalities must be distinguished in the islands, in addition to the scattered bands of Negritos and more or less Negritoid Hill people. All of these differed in speech; invariably they also differed more or less in customs. Most of the distinctions of custom are striking rather than deep-seated; but the divergence between the Christian, Mohammedan, and pagan tribes is profound. This classification, therefore, offers the best approach for a review of the peoples of the Philippines. (Map 6.)

The Tagalog of central Luzon are the best-known and most advanced nation among the Christians;

in fact, of all the peoples of the islands. Numbering somewhat short of two millions, they are only
the second largest nationality. But the location of
the capital city, Manila, in their territory, and their
general proximity to this center of government and
civilization, have thrown in their way many advantages which have reached the other nationalities in
more diluted form. Not only is education among
the mass of people probably most advanced among
the Tagalog, but they possess the most abundant
native literature, and their language is accepted as
the most elaborate and polished.

The largest nationality are the Bisaya of the
Bisayan or central islands. They were the people
first discovered in the Philippines, Magellan landing
and meeting his death among them in 1521. The
first Spanish attempts at subjugation were also di-
rected against them. They number four millions or
more than two-fifths of the total population. The
Spaniards of the early period knew them as Pintados or "painted people," owing to their fondness
for tattooing the body. Their numbers have grown
very rapidly and they are showing an increasing inclination to spread out from their native islands to
the coasts of Mindanao and Palawan. While
slightly less advanced in civilization, on the whole,
than the Tagalog, their superior numbers put them
in a position which leaves the probable ultimate predominance among the many nationalities of the
islands between these two.

Situated between the Tagalog and the Bisaya, and
on the whole affiliated more closely with the latter,
although situated in southern Luzon, are the Bikol,
also a considerable people, numbering about two-
thirds of a million.

To the north of the Tagalog, the first Christian nation encountered are the Pampanga in the fertile lowlands of the river and province of this name. They became ready converts to Christianity and Spanish rule, and the early records abound with praises of the bravery and fidelity for which they were distinguished among the native soldiers in the service of the King of Spain.

Beyond, in the Province of Zambales, are the Sambal, somewhat off the main tracks of communication, and subjugated considerably later than the other Christian peoples. As might be expected, they therefore lag somewhat behind in their general advancement. They are also much the smallest of the recognized Christian nationalities.

Farther north are the Pangasinan, also in the province of the same name. The Spaniards had trouble with them at first, but they have long since joined the other converts and are now prosperous in their rich bottomlands.

Along the narrow strip of coast known as North and South Ilocos are the Ilokano, a million strong, and the third greatest people in the islands. The Ilocos coast was rather heavily populated at the time of discovery, and has long since proved insufficient to hold the entire mass of this people. They have spread southward and eastward along the coast, and up and down the larger river valleys, encroaching upon the Sambal, Pangasinan, and Cagayan, often assimilating them and threatening ultimately to extinguish them. They are easily the most restless and inclined to move of all Philippine peoples. These habits are very likely left over from the period when their numbers were over-concentrated in a small area. They and the Pangasinan approach most closely of all Filipinos to the specifically Mongolian type of body. This may seem a very natural condition in view of their being geographically nearest to China, but the proportion of Chinese now settled in the Ilokano and Pangasinan districts is small, and historical records of the Chinese establishing themselves on these coasts in unusual numbers seem somewhat conflicting.

The home of the people usually called Cagayan, although their language is known as Ibanag, is the valley of the Cagayan, the greatest river in Luzon and the archipelago. They have yielded certain parts of their territory to the Ilokano. With them there must be included, on a broader view, the Christianized portion of a people whose pagan members are still reckoned as distinct, the Gaddang of the higher courses of the Cagayan.

The Batanes, the inhabitants of the islands of the same name, halfway between Luzon and Formosa, speak a language of their own whose affiliations have sometimes been placed with the Ilokano and sometimes with Cagayan.

The Isinai have maintained themselves only in three towns in Nueva Vizcaya. While a separate people, they may also be reckoned as members of the Ilokano group. The same, it may be remarked, can be said of many of the pagan mountaineers of Luzon; at least so far as their speech goes.

In a broader view, the foregoing nationalities are remarkably alike. There are towns, roads, and permanently cultivated fields in their territories, settled administration, schools, and devout adherence to Catholicism. Slavery has long gone out of use in form, but peonage, its economic substitute, prevails in many districts. The poor become the debtors and dependents of the rich. The men wear trousers and shirts; the women gowns of cotton, or where they can afford the expense, of beautiful textiles woven of pineapple fiber with or without silk. The amusements are church festivals, cock fighting, and gambling.

Much the greater part of the regions now Christian was subdued by the Spaniards within a few years after their first landing. The land and natives were parceled out into *encomiendas,* some of which went to the king or the church, but the majority to soldiers in the subjugating army. These men practically became feudal barons to whom the natives of their district paid tribute. A list of *encomiendas* and tributes made out in 1591, only twenty-five years after the Spaniards began their conquest, shows a large number of settlements which have persisted under the same name to the present time. The population was much smaller than now; but the nationalities were distributed substantially as at present, and with their relative strength approximating more closely to modern conditions than might be expected.

	1591	1916
Bisaya	168,000	3,977,000
Tagalog	124,000	1,789,000
Ilokano	75,000	989,000
Bikol	77,000	685,000
Pangasinan (only partly reduced)	24,000	381,000
Pampanga	75,000	337,000
Cagayan (perhaps overestimated, and including Gaddang, etc.)	96,000	156,000

Mohammedan Peoples. The Mohammedan peoples have been conspicuous in Philippine history for their propensity to war and piracy, and the fact that they maintained their independence unbroken until near the end of the period of Spanish occupancy. Even then they were only half subdued, and were largely left by the Spaniards to their own devices. But in numbers they have always been weaker than the Christians. Today there are but little over three hundred thousand Mohammedans in the archipelago as against more than eight million Christians. In fact, the Mohammedans are outnumbered more than two to one by the pagans. They have remained almost wholly restricted to southern Mindanao and the Sulu chain of islands. The Spaniards applied to them the name Moros, "Moors," which, of course, meant nothing but Mohammedans. The designation has however stuck, and inasmuch as the Mohammedan tribes are all very similar in customs and in their attitude toward the foreigner, it remains a convenient group name.

It is true that the Moro are not wholly uniform, especially on the side of language; but the differences between them have not been primarily ethnic, as in the remainder of the Philippines, but political. The Mohammedan introduced, along with his religion, the idea of the sultanate or kingship, and the native who embraced Islam soon came to think of himself as a follower of such and such a lord or over-lord, with his residence in this or that little capital, rather than as a member of one or another nationality. The fluctuating fortunes of the sultanates rested very largely on the personal character and abilities of the temporary occupant of the throne. The most important states were those of Sulu and of Cotabato or Magindanao. The latter was situated at the mouth of the great Magindanao

River from which the island of Mindanao is named, and up which the Mohammedan faith penetrated a considerable distance. Another center of Moro settlement was in the district of Lake Lanao in the narrow middle region of Mindanao.

One Mohammedan people must be specially mentioned, the Samal, often known as the sea gypsies from their wandering maritime habits. Tradition brings them from Johore in the Malay Peninsula. Whether or not this is authentic, numbers of the same or a similar people frequent the shores of various of the East Indies. They live either on the immediate shore or outright on their boats, and do not practise agriculture, but derive their living from fishing, trade, or piracy. Those settled on the coast are distinguished as the Samal proper or "companions;" the dwellers in boats are the Bajao or Samal Laut, the "sea people." Both groups generally acknowledged the suzerainty of the sultan of Sulu and furnished the mainstays of the crews on his expeditions. They are an extremely interesting people of whose inner mode of life very little is known.

Pagan Tribes. The modern pagans of the Philippines fall into two large bodies and a few comparatively insignificant ones. One great mass occupies the mountainous interior of northern Luzon; the other, the larger part of the heavily forested interior of Mindanao. Both regions are hinterlands which Christianity as well as Mohammedanism long failed to penetrate. In fact, parts of both regions rest unexplored to the present day. The Spaniards made but half-hearted and gradual efforts to establish themselves among these heathen, although the priest often preceded the captain and the governor.

Several of the pagan tribes remained practically unknown until after the American occupation.

These two groups of pagans, who aggregate about two-thirds of a million or twice as much as the number of American Indians surviving in the United States, are of the greatest interest in that they undoubtedly reveal to us the approximate condition in which all the Filipinos lived at the time of discovery. The resemblance of their society, arts, and religion, in spite of the separation of the two masses by many hundreds of miles of sea and land, is really very great. There can thus be no doubt that the intervening peoples, such as the Bisaya and Tagalog, must have shared in this community of culture. A study of the Bontok or Bagobo therefore illuminates at innumerable points the rather cursory records which the early Spaniards left concerning the peoples now Christianized.

There is, however, one difference observable between the pagans of Luzon and those of Mindanao. This is the kind and degree of their exposure to foreign influences in the pre-Spanish period. The inland districts of Mindanao seem to have absorbed somewhat more from Hindu civilization than those of Luzon. It cannot be affirmed outright that this was due to the greater proximity of Mindanao to Borneo, and through it to Java and other western centers of early culture; for the Tagalog language, whose home is in Luzon, contains a larger proportion of Sanskrit words than any other. At some time or other, Hindu influences must therefore have reached Luzon as well as Mindanao and without first traversing the latter island. This being so, there seems no reason why the pagans of Luzon should not have absorbed as much of this higher civilization as the mountaineers of Mindanao. They were indeed unquestionably affected in some measure; but why they did not succumb more completely, is an unexplained fact. The reason may possibly be sought in topography. The interior of Luzon is exceedingly rugged, whereas Mindanao is traversed by only one large mountain chain and contains two great river systems.

Then, at a later period, but still before the arrival of Europeans, came the Mohammedan advent. This proceeded from Borneo or followed its coasts and launched itself upon the Sulu Islands and western and southern Mindanao. It had only just begun to reach some outposts in Luzon when the Spaniards put an end to the propaganda. The wild tribes of Mindanao however continued to receive many articles in trade from the Moros, and even those who remained thoroughly pagan adopted something of their skill in working steel and brass, and their weapons and clothing. Of the two regions, then, Luzon is somewhat more representative of the rude civilization that prevailed over the Philippines a thousand or two thousand years ago.

Pagans of Luzon. The most northerly pagan group in Luzon are the Apayao, who are perhaps the least known of any. They are situated between the Ilokano and Cagayan; in speech and therefore origin they are said to incline more to the latter. In physique, they are transitional between the Indonesian and Malayan sub-races.

To the southwest of them, on the slopes toward the China Sea, are the Tinggian, who may be considered as little more than un-Christianized Ilokano, fairly representative today of the Ilokano of four centuries ago. They resemble the Christian Ilo-

kano in bodily proportions; and have received from
them certain elements of civilization, especially of
a material kind, which put them somewhat in ad-

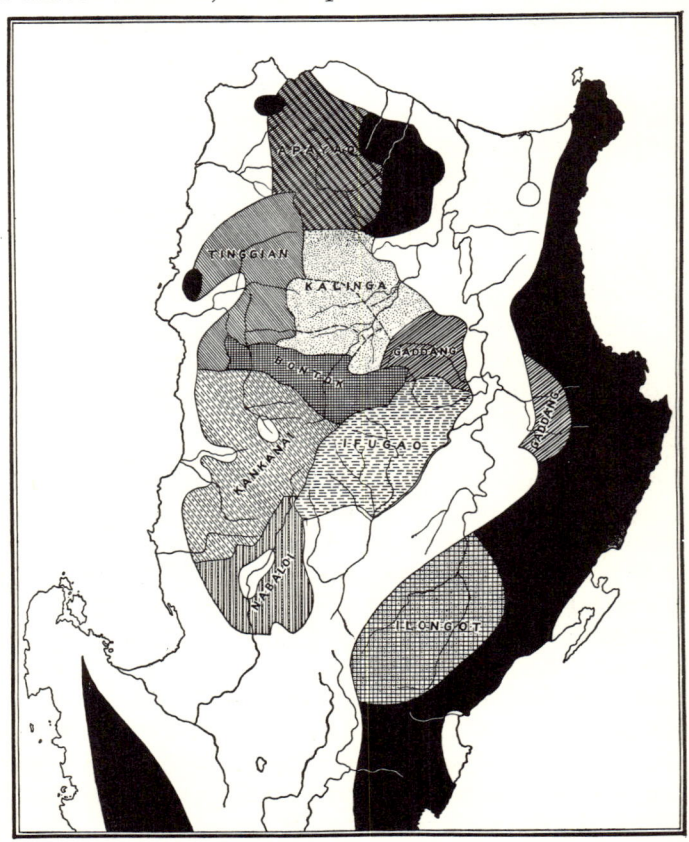

Map 4.   PAGANS OF NORTHERN LUZON.
Brown peoples in shading and named; Negritos in black; Christians in white.

vance of most of the other pagans.   They are a
scrupulously cleanly people.

To the south of the Tinggian live three groups of

people, the Bontok, Kankanai, and Nabaloi, who are often spoken of collectively as Igorot. The latter term has been used with a great variety of meanings. Some authorities, including the American census of 1903, make "Igorot" embrace all the pagans of northern Luzon, except the Negritos; others restrict it to the three tribes mentioned; whereas still others include only the Kankanai and Nabaloi. The term is therefore best avoided whenever possible. There is the more justification for such avoidance since the name means nothing more than "Mountain People." The Bontok are named after one of their towns which happened to be chosen as the seat of government for the district. Headhunting was in full swing at the time of the arrival of the Americans; but like all the other pagans, the Bontok accepted American rule kindly and almost cheerfully. While often irked by the enforcement of the law against feuds and head-taking, they appreciate the advantages of security, and seem to resent American authority much less than the attempts at Spanish rule and the guidance of the Christianized Filipino. The Bontok are to date the best-known pagan people of Luzon, and appear to have developed certain peculiarities such as the institution of the *ato,* a local division or ward within the town. To the south of the Bontok are the Kankanai with a large territory, and beyond them, the Nabaloi, often known as the Benguet Igorot. Spanish influence became rather strong among these people toward the end of the nineteenth century, but they have succeeded in maintaining many of their old habits and nearly all of their religion. Of the three groups, the Bontok are the most, and the

Nabaloi the least numerous; taken together, they aggregate well over a hundred thousand people.

Eastward of the last are the Ifugao—the word means "people" or "hill-people"—a group living packed together in the subprovince of the same name, to the estimated number of 132,000. The system of growing irrigated rice on terraces built up the mountain sides and watered by ditches heading in the river miles above—a system followed by most of the pagans of Luzon—reaches its greatest development among the Ifugao, some of their engineering works being truly astounding. The terraces are sometimes forty feet in height and less than that in breadth, so that the labor involved in the construction of a small field is enormous. Like most of their neighbors, the Ifugao are exceedingly industrious, working at their agriculture with an assiduity in which the Christian Filipino rarely attempts to share. They are broken up into innumerable small groups which were constantly in feud with each other. But with all the unsettlement of daily life they have worked out an elaborate and interesting system of law.

North of Bontok and Ifugao lives a miscellaneous assemblage of tribes usually thrown together under the group name Kalinga, which means nothing more than "enemy." They are about half as numerous as the Ifugao, and the second largest pagan group in the islands. The Kalinga are exceedingly heterogeneous. Their customs differ markedly from locality to locality, and their idioms appear to vary no less. It seems that at least five principal groups of Kalinga can be recognized. An attempt to indicate these subdivisions has been made on the map. The original affiliations of the Kalinga as a whole seem

to have been with the Cagayan, as might be expected
from their residence on streams which drain directly into the Cagayan River. Southeastward
from them are the remnants of the "wild Gaddang."
It is possible that when fuller information becomes
available these should be included as a Kalinga division.

One other pagan group remains in Luzon, the
Ilongot of the extreme headwaters of the Cagayan,
where they border on the Ilokano and the Tagalog
of the province of Nueva Ecija. They are separated from all the preceding wild tribes by tracts
that are either uninhabited or settled by Christians.
The territory of the Ilongot is rugged and has been
only partially explored. They live in much scattered small units and their numbers are limited,
probably not exceeding six thousand. As might be
expected under these conditions, they are ruder in
their habits than almost all the other heathens.

Pagans of Mindanao. In Mindanao the pagan
people are cut into two masses by the intrusive
Moros of Lake Lanao. The smaller western section
is inhabited by the Subanun or "River People,"
some thirty thousand in number. East of Lake
Lanao, in fact stretching down to the narrow strip
of eastern coast colonized by the Bisaya, are two
large groups, the Bukidnon, estimated to number
nearly fifty thousand, and the Manobo in the valley
of the Agusan, about forty thousand strong. On
the headwaters of the Agusan lives a small and almost unknown tribe, the Manguangan. South of
them, on the peninsula east of the Gulf of Davao,
are a better-known group, the Mandaya. North and
west of the Gulf in the interior are the Ata, and
nearer the coast, the Bagobo. The latter are the

Mindanao tribe on whom there is fullest information. To the south, in the Sarangani Peninsula, there live three tribes, the Bilaan, highest in the mountains; next, the Tagakaolo; and below them, the Kulaman; while Moros are settled on the immediate coast. On the map, these groups create a striking impression of a stratification of population. It is possible that when the distribution of these four nationalities has been worked out more in detail, it will prove to be less regular in its arrangement of concentric bands. It is doubtful how far the position of these peoples represents actual successive immigrations, or on the other hand a mere infiltration of alien customs from the seaboard.

Somewhat to the west of the last groups, and separated from them by Moros or by uninhabited tracts, are the Tirurai. Their affiliations seem to be with the eastern tribes rather than with the Subanun. Like most of the uncivilized peoples of southern Mindanao, they are not very numerous.

Pagans of Other Islands. There remain pagans of considerable interest on two other islands: the Tagbanua or "people of the country" in Palawan, and the Mangyan or "savages" in Mindoro. Both are exceedingly interesting backward peoples who have yielded most of the shores of their islands to intrusive Moros, Bisaya, and Tagalog, but have retained a culture which on the whole is perhaps simpler than that which prevailed among most of the natives four hundred years ago. Their dress is scant, agriculture and the iron industry little developed, and the population very sparse over the considerable areas involved. It is very remarkable that with such a general low culture both the Tagbanua and Mangyan should have succeeded in pre-

serving forms of the old native alphabet of Hindu
origin which once prevailed through the greater
part of the islands but has everywhere else yielded
to the Roman or Arabic systems of writing. The
writing is done by incising bamboo, but a difference
in the direction of the script used by the Tagbanua
and Mangyan indicates that the two tribes preserved their alphabets independently of each other.

In addition to the groups here enumerated are the
several bodies of Negritos and of the more or less
Negritoid Hill people who are practically unknown,
and some of whom, such as those of Samar and perhaps Panay, may prove to be nearly pure Malaysians: in which case they would be placed among the
groups here discussed.

It is notable that both the Hill people and the Negritos, in spite of their exceeding backwardness,
often live very close to well civilized peoples, so far
as distance in miles goes. The gap which separates
them from civilization is therefore one of habits and
habitat, rather than of absolute distance. Twenty-
five or thirty miles out of Manila or Iloilo suffices to
bring one into the territory of such bush people.
A few miles out of the clearings and one stands in
a mountain jungle rarely frequented by any human
soul other than those retiring and elusive savages
who are forever conscious of the difference between
themselves and civilized men and unwilling to
bridge the gap by more than occasional communica-
tions.

CHAPTER II

SPEECH

EACH of the many Philippine tribes or nationalities talks a language of its own, and some have their proper speech divided into several dialects. But all these tongues without exception go back to a common root form. This basis of Philippine speech recurs in Malay, as well as in the numerous languages of Celebes, Borneo, Java, Sumatra, and the smaller islands. The same fundamental tongue spread, at some remote time, northward to Formosa, and even across the vast breadth of the Indian Ocean to Madagascar off the shores of Africa.

Popularly, this generic East Indian speech, or rather language basis, is known as Malay, but in reality Malay is only one of some hundreds of local forms into which it has gradually diversified. At no great interval before the Portuguese discovery, the Malay proper, with his home on the Asiatic peninsula now named after him, had become converted to Islam, taking over with the new religion a superior political capacity and a restless, propagandizing spirit. These qualities carried him, as conqueror, pirate, trader, or settler, to the shores of many of the East Indian islands—Mindanao is an example—in which until then the kindred natives had lived with much less contact with the outside world. The Malay dialect thus became associated with the spread of Mohammedanism, and established as the language of commerce and diplomacy. This dominance led to its name being applied to the entire mass of languages of which it was only one member, although in certain respects the most conspicuous. On the side of literary achievement, Javanese, especially in its ancient Sanskrit-impregnated form known as Kawi, has a much more illustrious history. The position of Malay proper in its group may be compared to that of Attic Greek, which was also a late form as against the mass of Hellenic dialects, but became important through the political, commercial, and intellectual dominance of Athens. The relation of Latin to the ancient Italic tongues is another parallel.

But Malay has not yet replaced and perhaps never will replace the allied local languages to the same extent as Attic and Latin submerged their congeners; and a case in point occurs in the Philippines. The Moros of Sulu and Magindanao possess traditions, written in Arabic characters, that begin with the creation but soon pass from the domain of religion and fanciful legend to that of genealogy, carrying the thread to the present day. These records credit the introduction of Islam and the establishment of the local sultanates to Malays who came from Johore in the Malay peninsula to northern Borneo and the southern Philippines toward the close of the fourteenth century, or less than two hundred years before the Spanish conquest. This date agrees well with all that is known as to the period of Mohammedan spread and Malay expansion, and tallies also with the conditions which the first Spaniards found in the Mindanao region. If now these Malays, who reached the Philippines only five or six centuries ago, had come in numbers, they would undoubtedly have retained their speech and probably imposed it on many of the natives, as they did succeed in imposing Mohammedanism. As a matter of fact, however, the language of Sulu, Magindanao, etc., is in every case a local Philippine dialect, allied most closely to the languages of the pagans of Mindanao, and next to Bisayan. A few Malay words have crept into Sulu and Magindanao, and a certain proportion of the natives of these districts speak Malay in addition to their proper dialects, just as many Englishmen, Dutchmen, and Chinese in the East Indies have learned it because of its widespread utility in commerce.

In short, the fortunes of the invading Mohammedan Malay and Catholic Spaniard in the south and north of the Philippines were exactly the same. Each established his rule and religion and introduced new political and economic conditions. Both failed to establish their own speech among the mass of the resident population because this population was infinitely more numerous than their conquerors.

There is no satisfactory name for the generic East Indian form of speech, or the great group of Malaysian languages—the mother tongues of more than fifty million human beings—as distinguished from the one proper Malay language. Philologists have got into the habit of calling the group Indonesian; which would be satisfactory if some anthropologists did not employ Indonesian to designate precisely the proto-Malaysian or primitive Malaysian racial type which they distinguish on many of the islands from the historic Malayans. It is the languages of the latter—Malay, Javanese, Tagalog, and so forth—that the philologist chiefly has in mind when he says Indonesian. This word is therefore dangerously ambiguous unless clear specification is made in every case whether reference is to race or to speech.

It must be admitted that philologists have not yet been able to find a basic distinction in speech corresponding to the racial stratification into the primitive and later Malaysian types. Both types occur in Borneo, but all the tongues of that island are primarily Bornean and ultimately Malaysian, without aligning in any way as their speakers do into a more and a less Mongoloid group. The same is true in the Philippines. The Bontok in Luzon and the Bagobo in Mindanao are, physically, proto-Malayan; the Ilokano and the Sulu belong to the second racial stratum. Now everything would be much simpler, and our theories of racial and historical development ever so much stronger, if Bontok and Bagobo proved to be only variants of one primary division of East Indian speech, and Ilokano and Sulu common members of another. The reverse is actually the case. Bontok and Ilokano affiliate, and again Bagobo and Sulu. The speech of the primitive and later types on the same island is more closely related than the speech of two primitive— or two later—groups on different islands. In short, so far as language relations are concerned, geographical position and not adherence to a particular racial type is clearly the determining factor.

A classification of the Philippine languages among themselves reveals at least five larger groups.

1. Northeastern Luzon: Ibanag (Cagayan), Gaddang, Kalinga, Apayao, Ilongot.

2. Northwestern Luzon: Ilokano, Pangasinan, Tinggian, Bontok, Kankanai, Nabaloi, Isinai, probably of Ifugao; perhaps Sambal.

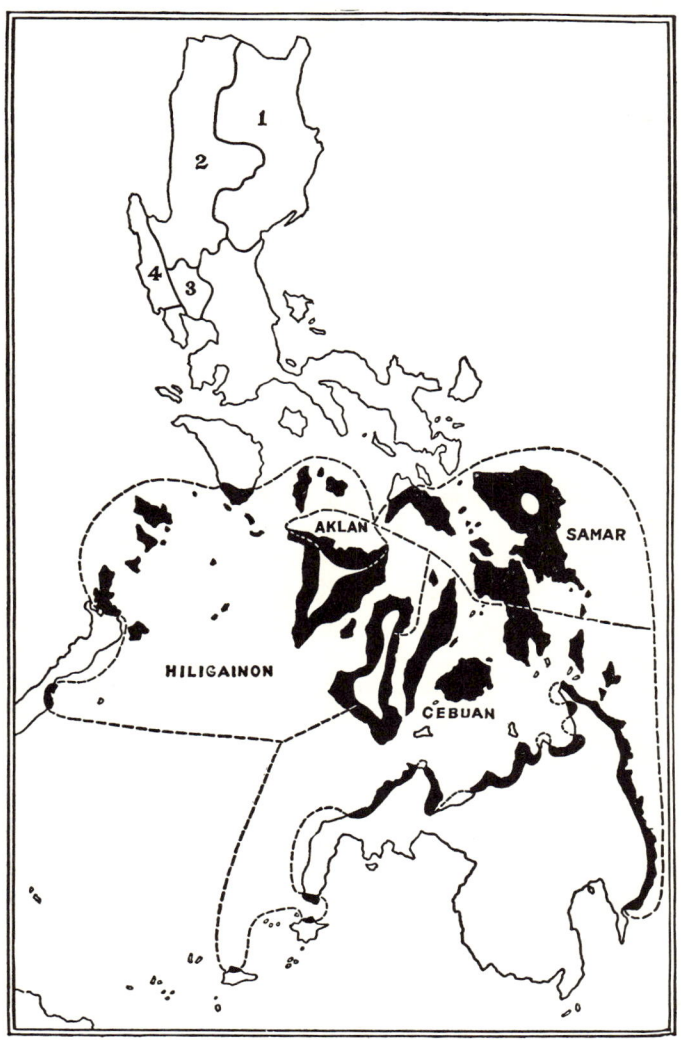

Map 5.   SOME PHILIPPINE LANGUAGES.

Four divergent dialect groups of northern Luzon : 1 Cagayan type ;
2 Ilokano type ; 3 Pampanga ; 4 Sambal (doubtful) ; and the four principal varieties of the Bisaya tongue (distribution in black) ; showing
the diversification of speech in land areas and its unchanged spread
by sea.

3. North Central Luzon: Pampanga—perhaps a diversified offshoot from the last or next.

4. Central region: Tagalog, Bikol, Bisaya.

5. Mindanao. The languages of this island are too imperfectly known to allow of their certain placing. They show some similarities to Bisaya, but may constitute a distinct group, or even more than one.

The position of the languages of Palawan and Mindoro, as of Sambal, remains obscure.

While some of these idioms, such as Tagalog, are very well known, there is no information on others beyond brief vocabularies, and in regard to several dialects nothing at all has been published. The classification is therefore tentative; but in its main outlines it promises to stand. Its most significant feature, well brought out by the map, is the tendency toward specialization and diversification in the north of the archipelago. Three of the five groups of tongues are confined to the northern half of the island of Luzon: and as for the remaining two, it is not even certain that they are distinct. Topography may be responsible. The central cordillera of Luzon, in whose region the Northeastern and Northwestern groups adjoin and from which Pampangan is not far removed, is easily the most intricate and irregular mountain system in the Philippines, in which trade is restricted and communication painfully slow even today. Nature has thus provided unusual opportunity for local dialects to spring up and become accentuated.

It is clear in every way that intercourse within the archipelago occurred much more readily by sea than by land even at an early period. A striking example is furnished by the Bisayan dialects, whose areas are outlined in Map 5. Different dialects are spoken on the two sides of single islands of no great size; whereas a single dialect extends across straits or seas to the confronting shores of other islands. The distribution of Tagalog and Bisaya on Mindoro points to the same condition. Only Ilokano seems to reflect a different story; but this tongue had no other islands opposed to its original seat of development, and therefore appears to have sidled along the coasts of northern Luzon until it could spread no farther, and then to have pushed up two or three large open river systems during the last century. On the other hand Ilokano has spread comparatively little into its own immediate hinterland, which is mountainous.

On a wider view, it became apparent to scholars a century ago that all the East Indian languages bore abundant traces of a common origin with those of the Polynesian islands, far out in the Pacific. To this great family, usually denominated the Malayo-Polynesian, and sometimes of late the Austronesian, the Melanesian and Micronesian tongues of the nearer parts of the Pacific were also found to belong. With the exception of New Guinea, and Australia somewhat off to one side, all the languages of Oceania are therefore only varieties of one fundamental stock, the vast sweep of which reaches from Hawaii and Easter Island, fronting the coast of America, to Madagascar near South Africa, or more than half way around the planet.

More recently it has been accepted by some students that the Mon-Khmer and other languages of Indo-China, the Sakai and Semang of the Malay Peninsula, the Khasi of Assam, and the Munda of India proper, form part of a great assemblage, the

Austro-Asiatic. Some go further and think they can see an ultimate connection between this Austro-Asiatic group and the Malayo-Polynesian or Austronesian one, and have proposed the name Austric —"southeastern"—for the wider combination. The significance of the inclusion lies in the fact that, if sound, it brings the Malayo-Polynesian stock definitely on to the Asiatic mainland, and so suggests possible origins that remained obscure as long as the family seemed to be wholly oceanic and insular.

Philippine speech thus is only a minute fragment of a widening series of circles: East Indian, Malayo-Polynesian, possibly Austric. Its ultimate problems are problems of these greater groups. Where language is common or akin, there must have been communication, perhaps original unity of the speakers; and with speech, something of culture must have flowed from one region to another. It is in these vast perspectives that the languages of the Philippines find their setting and their illumination.

Chapter III

THE MATERIAL SIDES OF LIFE

Agriculture and Domestic Animals. There is a widely prevalent theory that mankind as a whole has passed through three successive stages with reference to its food. According to this view, people were first hunters, fishermen, or gatherers of roots and berries; after a time they came to domesticate animals and lead a pastoral life; in the last state, they are reputed to have added the domestication of plants, in other words, agriculture.

This theory rests upon two foundations. The first is the observation that all nations of hunters possess a comparatively rude civilization—always, at any rate, inferior to that of Europeans. The second prop to the theory is the knowledge that the Hebrews and certain European peoples changed from the pastoral to the agricultural life about the beginning of the historical period. It will be seen that these two facts are a very slender foundation on which to rear a hypothesis applicable to mankind in general. Indeed, it has long since been noted that there are so many contrary cases that the theory must be looked upon as untenable. In the whole of aboriginal America, for instance, animals other than the dog were domesticated in only a few places and at best utilized only to a subsidiary extent. In a large part of both North and South America, however, agriculture was practised, in many regions intensively, and there can be no doubt whatever that this mode of life was entered directly from the hunting and root-gathering stage.

81

Domestic animals are kept in most parts of the East Indies, but always among people that also till the soil and in every case place more dependence on their crops than on their pigs and fowls. In fact, the breeding of animals is so universal an accompaniment of agriculture, and so distinctly secondary to it throughout Oceania, that there is hardly any conclusion possible but that it was developed as a side-product of agriculture and probably subsequently to the latter.

The problem therefore shifts from the general but erroneous theory, to the question of how the transition from a hunting to a farming life was accomplished in the Philippines and East Indies. In the nature of the case, such a transition may happen more easily in the fertile tropics than in more temperate latitudes. The breadfruit tree, the banana, the coconut palm, to take only a few examples, require only the slightest attention to make them yield useful food for many years. For other crops, such as the sweet potato, which is grown so abundantly in the Philippines, the procedure is little more difficult. All that plants of this type need to produce a bountiful crop is a clearing to give them a start, and some protection against the natural growths that threaten to choke them out of existence. Many of the difficulties that confronted and must often have discouraged the incipient agriculturist in more northern latitudes are therefore scarcely present in the tropics.

If then agriculture can be slid into, as it were, by even lowly tribes, it is hopeless to look at the present time for a precise knowledge of the very first beginning of the art in the Philippines. Our best evidence lies in the plants cultivated—the areas in which these are native in the wild state, and the historic peoples known to have possessed them longest. The facts of this order show without exception that agriculture was introduced into the Philippines ready-made; not one of the food plants is native to the islands. The problem of origins therefore becomes an extra-Philippine one.

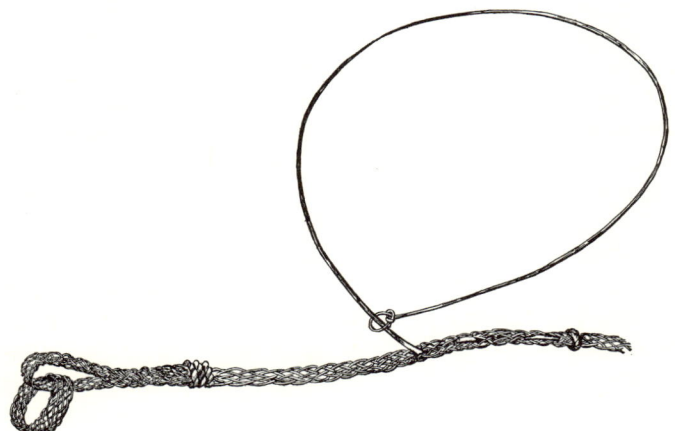

Fig. 11. Hunting Snare. Mangyan.

The presence in the Philippines of some bands of Negritos that do not farm, does not in any way antagonize this conclusion or seriously complicate the situation. Just in proportion as the majority of natives became dependent upon agriculture, they would require less territory for their maintenance. That territory would also tend to be concentrated in the lowlands, leaving the mountains and denser forests of little use or interest to them. This condition in turn would leave these wilder tracts wholly at the disposal of the less numerous hunting peoples, and so enable these to live without being seriously pressed for subsistence. In this way it is conceivable that the establishment of agriculture might itself incline for a very long time to perpetuate the hunting stage in closely adjacent regions. This conclusion is particularly applicable to the Philippines, where we know that the bulk of the population has long been concentrated on the coast.

As regards domesticated animals, it is notable that the Filipino kept only three besides the dog. These are the common fowl, the pig, and the carabao or water buffalo. All three of these varieties also occur wild on the islands, the chicken as the jungle fowl, the pig probably as a variety originally wild, whereas the buffalo has been introduced by man. Cattle and sheep were not known in the Philippines until after the arrival of the Europeans. Horses and goats are bred by some of the natives of Mindanao, but there is every indication that these were introduced by the Mohammedans, or at the utmost during the last phase of the period of Hindu influence.

The buffalo is now used both as a draught animal and for riding, but there seems to be no record of its being kept for any other purpose than food in the pre-European period. In fact, wheeled vehicles were unknown and roads on which they could have been used did not exist. Even today, the more remote pagans of Luzon keep their buffaloes only to slaughter them.

It is also not native practice in the Philippines to milk the buffalo or to utilize any dairy products. This is a habit characteristic not only of the East Indies, but of southeastern Asia.

Perhaps the most notable thing about the place of domesticated animals in primitive Filipino life is the fact that animals are rarely killed other than for a sacrifice, and that the flesh of sacrificed animals is consumed wholly or almost wholly by the worshippers. This seems to have been true of all the natives when discovered, and is still the custom of the uncivilized peoples. Since sacrifice is the most important act in ceremonial, it is clear that the Filipino thinks of eating flesh as essentially an accompaniment of religion, and conversely of religion —at least in all its greater and more public manifestations—as always ending in a substantial meal.

This devotion, in theory at least, of domestic animals to the purposes of religion, is likely to be an importation. The idea of animal sacrifice is cardinal in the religion of the ancient Greeks, Hebrews, and other nations in the region of the eastern Mediterranean. It is not essentially East Asiatic; or if ever it was, fell at an extremely early period into nearly complete disuse. The more or less uncivilized regions in which the life sacrifice still prevails, such as large parts of Africa, are so situated that the practice might easily have been introduced by diffusion from its original Mediterranoid center. There seems considerable probability that the sacrifice usages were also carried eastward from their earliest hearth, presumably through India, and thence to the East Indies and the Philippines. It does not of course follow necessarily that the breeding of animals was unknown before. But its identification with the sacrifice concept is so undeniably close today, that there exists the possibility that both traits of culture were carried into the Philippines as merely two aspects of a single set of practices.

Rice Culture. Rice is the staple food of the Filipino of every condition, and the thing that probably occupies his life-long attention more than any one other. His most regular labor is that which he performs in the cultivation of this plant. In place of money, he uses measures of rice, both as standards of value and in actual transfers. The greatest article of wealth among so thoroughly pagan a people as the Ifugao is the rice field. A man who inherits enough of these is thereby rich and his position in society established. Rice fields are the last of his possessions which an Ifugao willingly allows to pass from the tenure of his blood line. Every tribe whose religion has not broken down before Christianity or Mohammedanism, practices at least one important ceremony whose main purpose is the production of rice; frequently a whole series of such rituals are performed for each stage of rice agriculture—the clearing of the ground, the planting, the cultivation, the harvesting, and the preservation of the crop. It is significant that even though other crops are grown, they very rarely have special ceremonies devoted to them. The native point of view is clearly that if the success of the rice is insured by the necessary magical and ceremonial means, other crops will automatically take care of themselves. When plant food is offered to the spirits in any connection, it is almost invariably rice. In short, the Filipino not only eats rice, but thinks in terms of rice, and if his civilization is to be described in a single phrase it can only be named a rice culture.

Much more than a hundred varieties of rice are distinguished by the natives. But from the point of view of the student of Filipino life, these fall into two great classes; swamp rice, which can be grown only in marshes or under irrigation; and upland or mountain rice, which needs no watering beyond that supplied by the rains. The distinction between these two types is slight botanically—they are varieties of one species; but it is important because of

Fig. 12. Rice Terraces on Mountain Side; Flooded with Water. Itugao.

its effect on the habits of the people. Swamp rice keeps its cultivators in the lowlands, or forces them to construct irrigation works which become elaborate in proportion as the country follows rugged contours. Upland rice has a smaller yield, but possesses the advantage that it can be grown almost anywhere, and makes possible adherence to the *kaingin* system of scattered clearings in the forest.

Terrace Irrigation. Whereas it might be expected that the advanced Christian natives would be the ones to undertake the more tedious and difficult task of growing irrigated rice while the backward pagans would content themselves with the simpler upland product, the reverse is partly true. The majority of pagans in Luzon not only depend wholly on swamp rice, but do so under enormous natural disadvantages. The splendid irrigation systems of the Bontok, Nabaloi and adjacent groups, culminating in the really astounding works of the Ifugao, have never failed to elicit the wonder and admiration of observers. These terraces and ditches involve an amount of labor, for maintenance as well as con-

Fig. 13.   Nabaloi Women weeding a Terraced Rice Field.

struction, that is almost unparalleled among peoples who in other traits of civilization have remained as uncivilized as these mountaineers.

The immediate stimulus is no doubt the heavy

congestion of population, which in parts of Bontok, Ifugao, and Kalinga today attains to a hundred and more souls per square mile. Other tribes of Luzon, such as the Apayao, and most of the pagans of Mindanao, grow only upland rice; but in every such case the population is much smaller. The Apayao for instance hold a larger territory than the Ifugao with perhaps one-fifth of their population. And Mindanao as a whole appears always to have had not nearly as many inhabitants as Luzon. While loose groups like the Mandaya, Manobo, and Bukidnon each aggregate twenty-five to fifty thousand souls, these live much scattered over extensive stretches of country. The Bagobo area in Mindanao may be fairly compared with that of the Bontok or Ifugao; but the Bagobo population is estimated to be only one-seventh and one-fifteenth as great respectively.

However, numerous as they are, the Igorot and adjacent peoples are rude in their general culture, and the question therefore arises whether their fine irrigation system is an invention of their own or an importation; and if the latter, were its introducers they themselves when they first came to the Philippines, or some other people? As for the general question of local invention or importation, there can be little doubt. The idea of terrace irrigation was familiar to other Filipino groups and to many of the inhabitants of the East Indies generally. If nations like the Tagalog and Pampanga did not build the endless step fields of the Ifugao, it is because they possessed sufficient lowlands. The word Tagalog is said to mean, "those of the *alog*," the lands that are converted into marsh after a storm; Ilocano is from the same stem, *ilog*; and both the names Pangasinan and Pampanga are derived from *pang-an,* a river bank. Most of the Pampanga country, in fact, is a vast swamp in the rainy season and stands more in need of drainage than of having water fed into the fields. Almost everywhere along the immediate coast heavily watered lowlands were available. Elsewhere in Malaysia a similar condition prevails. In Java, which is a rather narrow and distinctly mountainous island, whose population early became heavy, the same thing occurs as in Luzon. There are too many people for the bulk of them to live actually on the river mouths. The majority therefore dwell at some elevation and farm on irrigated terraces. Moreover, the system of terraced irrigation is extensively followed in Japan, China, and Indo-China. On a broader view, therefore, the terraces of the Luzon mountaineers are by no means a unique phenomenon in their part of the world. They impress by their stupendousness and daring and by the contrast which they display with the general backward status of their makers; but their peculiar quality is one of intensity and not of kind.

Now the almost unanimous verdict of both history and ethnology is that when a certain art is shared by a number of peoples, and evidence as to its origin is obtainable, it almost always becomes clear that this origin occurred among the more advanced rather than the less advanced peoples of the group; or where both are now equally advanced in general civilization, than among that nation whose civilization is the oldest. On the basis of this well-established principle, it becomes practically certain that the Igorot or Ifugao was not the inventor of his system of irrigation. He undoubtedly extended it to conditions under which its pursuit has rarely been attempted by any other people; but the knowledge, the basic idea of the art, and the essentials of its technique, must have developed elsewhere. Where this center of origination lay, is another question which cannot be entered into here because it is a general Malaysian or East Asiatic problem and not a Filipino one: but the source is likely to have been on the mainland of southeastern Asia; or if in the East Indies, then in that portion of them nearest Asia.

It is more difficult to form a judgment as to who may have been the carriers of this invention to the interior of Luzon. Theoretically, it might have been the very ancestors of the wild people now settled there. But if so, they came from the higher center of civilization where the art of terracing took its origin. They might thus be expected to have brought along other achievements, such as writing or statecraft. Since they are deficient in these elements of culture, it follows that they must have suffered a degeneration in matters other than agriculture; and of such a decadence there is little indication.

It seems therefore distinctly more probable that the mountaineers of Luzon first settled in their present habitats and grew upland rice or other crops, or did not follow agriculture at all; and that subsequently the practice of growing part of their rice by irrigation became established through importation of the technique by more advanced peoples. As the mountain population increased, the new art became more and more valuable, and its practice was elaborated and perfected to a degree which the otherwise superior lowlanders did not attain, because necessity failed to spur them on.

It is rather in support of this interpretation that apart from its actual irrigation works, the Igorot and Ifugao rice culture is an excessively simple one. The work is all done by hand. The planter is nothing but a stick; seeding, transplanting, and weeding are all carried on with the fingers. The only tool employed by the Ifugao is a simple wooden shovel. Where the plow is used, it seems to be an adoption of Spanish usage.

Throughout the Philippines rice is stored either in the house or in thatched granaries. It is cooked in bamboo joints, in pottery vessels, or in iron kettles according to the general advancement and trade facilities of each group. Being as tasteless as it is a nourishing food, a great variety of vegetable condiments are used by every Philippine people to flavor their daily diet. It may be added that not only is there always a full set of names for each of the many varieties of rice, but that rice in the husk or on the stalk is invariably known by a different name from cooked rice, precisely as we distinguish wheat and flour or cattle and beef.

Various Food Plants. While rice is the representative food of the Philippines and the only one that has impressed native imagination, it is far from being consumed in such preponderance as its leading place and high estimation might suggest. In fact, rice seems to constitute rather less than half the total food eaten in the archipelago. In Mindanao, where irrigation was slightly developed but the equatorial climate provided an unusual variety of other useful plants, the first Spaniards reported that comparatively little rice was grown; and this condition has been maintained, at least in comparison to most of the islands. It is however true that the other food plants are of many kinds, and that any one of them alone is usually eaten to a less extent than rice.

The one crop that as regards quantity is a rival of rice, and in certain districts surpasses it, is the *camote* or sweet potato, *Ipomœa batatas*. This was introduced by the Spaniards from Mexico, is still known by its Aztec name, but spread rapidly to nearly all Philippine peoples. It requires much less care than rice, and can be grown, for a few years at least, on soil that would not yield the latter crop. Among the irrigating tribes that prize their rice terraces as their most valuable possessions, sweet potato fields are sold only for nominal sums such as the value of the standing crop. With the Nabaloi it is bad form to rent a *camote* field: the rich must grant its temporary use to the poor gratis.

Local conditions determine the varying proportions of rice and sweet potatoes consumed. Thus among the Ifugao, the rice grown in the Kiangan district is estimated to bear a proportion to sweet potatoes of 9 to 2; whereas in neighboring Banawe, the ratio is only 3 to 7.

But there is no question of the preference of the Filipino. The sweet potato soon palls as a steady diet, whereas rice becomes a habit like wheat, or even an article craved. The Ifugao reckons as *kadangyang* or rich only those families that grow enough rice to last them, even though eaten at every meal, the year round. The *mabitil* or middle class are those whose supply gives out before the next harvest is ripe. The poor or *nawatwat* use sweet potatoes as a staple, helped out perhaps by the rice which they manage to raise on some little patch, or which they receive as wages for tilling the fields of the wealthy.

In third place in Philippine agriculture maize is probably to be reckoned. This was of course introduced from America, but has long since formed an integral element of native farming, even among the most remote pagans who until recent years had never set eyes on a Caucasian, much less heard of the aboriginal American developers of the grain that they grew. The spread of useful plants is sometimes incredibly fast, especially in the tropics. Two hundred years sufficed to establish not only maize but tobacco and several other American plants through large parts of the East Indies, Asia, and Africa as firmly as if they were indigenous.

Of other annual crops, millet and the small varieties of beans were pre-Spanish, and are likely to have been introduced from Asia, perhaps in the first period of Hindu influence or even before. *Gabi* or taro is of rather more importance. It has a wide distribution in Oceania.

Of palms and trees yielding fruits or other edible products, the Philippines contain many varieties that have been made use of since the prehistoric period: the sago, coconut, breadfruit, durian, orange, lemon, lime, and banana being the principal.

The sago palm—its name is East Indian—is important especially in Mindanao. In 1582 it was reported to furnish the principal food supply on that island, where it is native.

The coconut palm was grown everywhere near the coast, but was of relatively less importance to the natives than in some of the smaller and more meagerly vegetated islands of the Indian and Pacific oceans. The same may be said of the breadfruit.

The banana group was of more consequence for the textile fiber—"Manila hemp"—taken from one of its small species, the abaca, than as a source of food yielded by the edible species.

Sugar cane was cultivated nearly everywhere when the Spaniards entered the islands. It was long one of the principal plantation crops; but the ancient Filipinos grew it for themselves in order to ferment from it a wine or rum. Such wine, made either from sugar cane or from rice or sometimes from the sap of the nipa palm, was consumed in large quantities by every tribe, but invariably as an accompaniment of religious feasting. There are some botanical indications that the original home of the sugar canes may have been New Guinea; and there they are cultivated today by rude tribes with simple agriculture.

The proportions of the subsistence of the Ifugao are computed to be as follows: Rice, 32 percent; sweet potatoes, 42; maize, 4; all other crops, 6; total from agriculture, 84; domestic animals, partly imported, 6½; small clams from the flooded rice fields, 8; all other game, fish, or wild plant foods, 1½. It is evident how insignificant animal breeding is in comparison with agriculture. This is undoubtedly true for all the pagan tribes, past and present. It is interesting that five-sixths of all the wild foods are constituted by the clams which are a by-product of the system of agriculture. With the Negrito, and among some groups advantageously situated for fishing, the ratio of wild foods no doubt rises considerably higher; but with these exceptions the figures seem to be generally representative. From eight to nine-tenths of what the Filipino consumes is the product of his farms.

Historically, agriculture is characterized by the fact that not even one of the many plants cultivated for food in the Philippines is botanically native to the islands. Manila hemp is the single cultivated species of consequence whose origin is indigenous. A certain number of ornamental or medicinal species have names of Sanskrit origin; a very few plants introduced by the Chinese have C h i n e s e appellations; considerably more are known by Spanish or Aztec designations—the latter due to Spanish importation from Acapulco in Mexico. What is true in this instance seems to be typical of Philippine culture as a whole: only a fraction is native to Malaysia, and but a little of this indigenous to the Philippines.

Tobacco and Betel. Tobacco was introduced by the Spaniards, and its growth fostered or enforced in certain districts. Even today Manila tobacco enjoys considerable repute. Most of the natives have become addicted to it. But the original equivalent was betel, whose use still maintains its priority among many tribes, especially the pagan and Mohammedan ones. Betel is chewed. It irritates the gums, turns the saliva blood red, and blackens the teeth; but the taste for it is apparently acquired easily and retains a firm hold. The essential element is the nut of the areca palm, *Areca catechu,* which is sliced, sprinkled with lime, and wrapped in a leaf of ikmo, *Piper betel.* The use of

Fig. 14. Incised Tube of Bamboo to hold Lime for Betel Chewing. Bagobo.

betel and tobacco products is not mutually exclusive, but tends to be, and clearly is, so far as connection with religion or formulated social custom is concerned.

In connection with the figures just cited, it may be mentioned that the number of acres devoted in 1903 to maize was a quarter of a million, to coconut three-eighths of a million, to "hemp," the chief export, over half a million, to rice between three and four millions.

Abacá and Cotton. The Spaniards found the natives cultivating two plants for use in spinning and weaving: cotton and the "Manila hemp" which has been mentioned as being in reality a small inedible species of banana, the *abacá, Musa textilis*. From the stalks of this, strong fibers are stripped which are much prized for civilized cordage. The Filipino wove and still weaves cloth from the fibers. The attractive textiles of the Bagobo are made in this material. Cotton was however of no less importance, and while its production in the islands is small because of a Spanish policy of discouraging or forbidding its cultivation in favor of tobacco and other monopolies, a number of pagan tribes still wear clothing of cotton. The Mangyan and some Ilokano and Tagalog grow the plant today. The Christian Filipino has added a new textile material, piña, that is pineapple leaf fiber introduced from America, from which valuable fabrics of beautiful semi-transparent finish are woven, both for men's and women's clothing. The Manila hemp plant is indigenous to the Philippines, and was probably first used as it grew wild. Cotton, on the other hand, does not seem to be native, and was in all likelihood imported from the western East Indies, whence in turn it may be derived from India proper, the region to which all indications point as the original home of cotton culture and manufacture.

Houses. The Filipino house is much the same among civilized and uncivilized tribes, and has changed but little since the islands were first visited by Europeans. It is a structure of wood or bamboo, with thatched roof, and floor raised above the ground. No traces of architecture in stone, either native, Hindu, or Mohammedan, have been found at any place in the archipelago. The Spanish edifices in Manila have several times suffered severely from earthquakes; yet it is not these seismic disturbances so much as his lack of cultural stimulation that kept the Filipino from construction in the more dignified and substantial material. Java, which is also severely shaken, is full of ruined Hindu temples, and Borneo is not without some traces. Had not the Philippines been so remote that the first force of Indian contact was spent before their shores were reached, we should undoubtedly find ancient stone buildings here also.

There is nothing very distinctive about the Filipino house. Its general type occurs through the forested tropical parts of the earth, at any rate wherever the population does not live clustered in cities. The main requisite is a steep roof to provide a dense shade from the sun and shed the torrential rains. The higher the peak, the better will the roof accomplish the latter purpose, besides drawing up under itself the hottest air in the interior. In a country of palms and luxuriant grasses, thatch is by far the most easily put on material and perhaps the most durable. The only drawback is the danger from fire; but with the building so easily replaced, the risk is felt to be rather toward inmates and property.

Fig. 15. Tree House. Gaddang.

The second requisite is a floor that shall be raised above the dampness of the ground and the snakes and vermin that infest its surface. The Filipino floor is always a few feet above the soil, often eight or ten, and sometimes, when houses are set in the forked branches of trees, twenty, forty, or even sixty feet.   The latter elevation of course serves no purpose other than protection from human enemies, and is only practicable among rude communities that live in isolated families or scattered local groups.   The tree house is an old institution in the Philippines.   It is still considerably used by the Gaddang and Kalinga in Luzon, by the Manobo and Mandaya of Mindanao, and even by some members of one Mohammedan group, the Moros of Lake Lanao, from whom comes the specimen exhibited in the Hall.   In spite of its picturesque appeal to the imagination, the tree house cannot be looked upon as being in principle more than a superficial

Fig. 16.   Moro Dwellings.   Except for being built over the water, the type is characteristic of Philippine houses generally.

modification of the one generic house type prevalent throughout the Philippines. The Bontok, Kankanai, and Nabaloi are the chief non-Negrito peoples in the Philippines to build directly on the ground.

The floor is most frequently made of bamboos, either split or in the round. For a hearth, a box of earth serves adequately, or a pottery vessel constructed for the purpose. Fire being required only for cooking, a small hearth is sufficient and a chimney unnecessary. Such smoke as there is rises under the thatched eaves. The space under the floor is often more or less enclosed, and during the day serves as a convenient place for the women to pound rice in the wooden mortar, while at night pigs or fowls may be kept there for protection. Some of the Luzon mountaineers perform sacrifices and hold the long death watch over the corpse beneath their house. If the ground space is not utilized for any of these purposes, it is generally because the posts on which the house rests are set in water or in soil which is periodically covered by the tides.

The least important parts of the house were its walls. Some of the ruder edifices, especially among the Negritos, occasionally lack these, the long gabled roof taking their place. Generally, rather low walls of thatch, bamboo slats, or wooden slabs are added. Windows are more frequent at present than in early times. The entrance is by a ladder of bamboo; in Cagayan, the shin bones of fallen foes were sometimes used as rungs. A porch or gallery at the level of the elevated floor often runs around the house. This is not customary among the mountain tribes even today, but early Spanish descriptions show it to be a native device. The interior is usually one large room. If compartments are present, they can generally be traced to Spanish influence. People of high rank, especially women, formerly sometimes let down a curtain of mats when they retired for the night.

The entire structure was put together without nails. The Filipino did not know this article; probably if he had known it, iron would have been too valuable to him to employ for a need that could be satisfied by lashings of rattan, or at most a little mortising. Where storms threatened, houses were often anchored to trees or the ground by lines of rattan.

In detail, there are of course innumerable variations of size, proportions, and materials from the general type described. Probably every nationality in the islands built a kind of house distinctive enough to be recognizable by the expert. But these differences are on the whole so superficial as to possess interest only for the specialist.

The large model of a house displayed in the Hall represents an average dwelling of the modern Christian native in the country districts. The uninhabited ground space is so heavily stockaded with bamboo as to give an impression of forming an integral part of the house, whereas in reality the single story is situated above it. The materials, thatching, ladder, verandah, windows, and shutters are representative.

The houses of the wealthy and even of chiefs did not differ from those of common men except for being larger and better built. The increase in size was usually in one direction only. Thus the chief's house, which served for public gatherings and ceremonies as well as for the domicile of the head man's family and retinue, was of nearly the usual breadth, but much longer. Such long houses are described in early sources for the Tagalog and are still used by the Bagobo.

Rice granaries were built in many districts, but in

others the harvest was stored in the living house. Groups of dwellings were often surrounded by stockades, as among the Tinggian. The Moro chiefs sometimes went so far as to build forts of wood or heavy bamboos, but this practice hardly prevailed outside of the Mohammedan regions.

Religious Structures. Other than the dwellings of their chiefs, the Filipinos seem to have known no public buildings, nor, strictly speaking, any edifices devoted to worship. The pagans sacrificed in the living house, under it, outdoors, or sometimes in thickets or groves. The practice of the now Christian nations seems to have been the same. Names for places of worship were recorded by the early missionaries in several dialects, but descriptions usually refer only to bowers, enclosures, or entirely open places, and the etymology of the terms would make them as applicable to any temporarily chosen spot of sacrifice as to a permanent structure devoted to the purpose. Thus the word *simbahan,* which the Tagalog now apply to a church, by no means implies that they possessed a corresponding ancient structure. In fact, the chief's long living house was so called during the period when it was in use for a ceremony.

There was one strictly religious building almost universally prevalent in the islands, the so-called spirit house. But this is too small for a congregation and often even for the officiating priest to enter. It is really not a house, but an altar in the form of a house and believed to be more or less frequented by spirits. Many of the pagan tribes, both northern and southern, still construct these little edifices in their fields and at other points. Invariably they have a roof resting on poles: walls and floor may be present or absent. Sometimes there are three walls, the fourth being left open. Tribal custom varies in these details. Plates, coconut bowls, or other receptacles are often set or hung inside. In these, offerings of food are deposited; or the priest may pray or recite a formula before or in the little structure. The ancient Tagalog at times erected these spirit houses inside their dwellings. They are described as having been set apart like a tower and entered over a little bridge of bamboo. Idols and other religious paraphernalia were kept in them. These spirit houses are one of the most characteristic features of Filipino religion, and the only type of ceremonial building well established in native usage.

Settlements. In general, the Filipino was not given to town life, or to clustering with his kind in considerable numbers. Even the capitals of the Mohammedan sultans often contained no more than two or three thousand souls. To the present day Manila remains the only large city in the archipelago. With all the development of industry and trade during three centuries of Spanish rule, there had grown up less than half a dozen settlements of ten thousand inhabitants or over when the Americans took possession. Cebu, when Magellan landed and the Spaniards first established themselves, is said to have contained five to ten thousand persons in the capital and environs. Not many years after, the town had shrunk considerably.

Among the modern non-Christian tribes there is considerable variety of usage as regards the size of villages. In Mindanao the custom is to live in small scattered groups. So numerous a people as the Ifugao follow the same practice, their houses, in spite of constant feuds, or perhaps because of them, being placed with reference to the fields. The Tinggian live more definitely in villages; and with the Bontok towns of a thousand people occur. However, this region of more concentrated villages is precisely the district in which the institution of the *ato* or ward within the town is developed. Inasmuch as governmental and religious functions inhere in the *ato,* the village as a whole is in reality little more than an accidental conglomeration of smaller units.

In the islands as a whole, irrespective of religion or degree of civilization, more than one-half of all the villages contain less than four hundred inhabitants, and half of the total population is resident in villages containing less than eight hundred persons. The "villages" referred to in these data are *barrios,* the smallest governmental unit recognized; in reality a *barrio* often contains a number of settlements, each bearing a name of its own. The number of actual villages is therefore considerably greater than the 13,400 *barrios* recognized, and the average population of each considerably less than the figures given would indicate.

General Character of Industries. The Christian Filipino is often charged with indolence, but those who first knew him frequently commended his industry. It is likely that the alteration in economic conditions, and a more modern standard of judgment, are responsible for the apparent change. The pagan peoples have never been accused of being lazy about their own occupations, and those of northern Luzon are universally described as extremely hard working, irrespective of sex or age.

Their method of agriculture is feasible only to consistently industrious people.

The Filipino is also quick to learn, like all East Indians, and adept with his hands; but it must be admitted that his manufactures lack pronounced artistic quality. He often finishes his work nicely; a clean job evidently appeals to him; yet he rarely goes farther or attempts to make his product positively beautiful. It is not that he leaves it ugly; but among other peoples of equal mechanical ability, skill flowers more often into specific aesthetic developments.

Bamboo and rattan are the materials most used in manufactures. Bamboo serves for receptacles, cooking vessels, spear shafts and heads, fire-making apparatus, musical instruments, boat rigging, and a variety of other objects, besides being used to an enormous extent in house construction. Rattan makes lashings and wrappings of all sorts, braided ornaments and bowstrings, the material of baskets, and generally is a substitute for cordage. Wood the Filipino employs considerably less, no doubt because it is harder to work than these two abundant and readily serviceable plants; but it enters into buildings and boats, weapon handles, bowls and spoons, looms, and the like. It is, however, rarely decorated; and the carvings of men and animals that occasional tribes make on their implements, or as figurines, are rather rude. The specific cause of this aesthetic poverty of woodwork may be the greater prevalence of technique developed in bamboo, which material lends itself naturally to incisions and etchings, but scarcely to true carving. None of the idols of the Tagalog and Bisaya has been preserved, but they appear to have been roughly made, perhaps not materially superior in artistic quality to those carved of porous fern root or stem by the modern Igorot tribes.

Animal skins, whether of the deer, wild boar, or domestic buffalo, are very little used by the Filipinos, and a proper tanning or dressing art can scarcely be said to exist.

Pottery. Pottery shares the just mentioned qualities. It is made almost universally, but is rarely ornamented, and usually strictly utilitarian. The original type is represented among the Bontok and the Subanun in Luzon and Mindanao. The clay is pulverized, moistened, and beaten or kneaded, without tempering material other than perhaps chopped grass. A lump is indented with the fist, and the hole pushed out from within, the other hand modeling the exterior or piecing on to the margin. The Tinggian work the clay while revolving it on a winnowing basket set on the ground. It is not clear whether this device is aboriginal or a degenerate potter's wheel imitated from the Christian Ilokano. The final shaping is done with a paddle that taps the outer surface while a smooth stone is held inside. Baking is in the open air, without a kiln, in a fire of dung, wood, or pine bark. The Bontok woman applies a resin to the red hot vessel, which produces a lustrous coating and renders the walls less porous. It is not a true glaze.

The Christian tribes now make a plain red ware that is surprisingly uniform among the various nationalities. If there is any decoration at all, it consists of slight patterns in white, or in a few incisions or relief additions. This ware is sometimes made by hand and sometimes on the potter's wheel.

The Moros manufacture glazed vessels, but it is

not known whether this is a true pottery glaze, imported along with the knowledge of firearms and other elements of Mohammedan culture, or an after treatment as in Bontok. The Moros also mark the surface into areas by means of incised lines and color these areas; but the color appears to be ap-

Fig. 17.   Red Jar with White Pattern, Bikol; Moro Jar with Lid.

plied after the pot is baked. At that, these feeble attempts represent the most that the Filipino has done in the way of beautifying his pottery.

This is the more remarkable because for centuries glazed and semi-porcelain wares have been imported from China and distributed throughout the Philippines, serving as the most precious heirlooms of the natives. All the pagan tribes possess such jars, which are carefully preserved for use as rice wine containers in great religious feasts, and are parted with only on the most important occasions, such as blood feud settlements or marriage contracts.

Morga wrote in 1609 of the Tagalog, Pampanga, Pangasinan, and Ilokano that "certain earthenware jars are found among the natives. They are very old, of a brownish color, and not handsome. . . . The natives are unable to give any explanation of where and when they got them, for now they are not brought to the islands, or made there. The Japanese seek and esteem them . . . and keep them in brocade cases." Similar vessels went to Borneo, where certain types maintained a value, until recently, of $1500 to $3000.

This imported ware, which the natives frequently do not recognize as Chinese but attribute to the gods or the beginning of the world, dates from the Sung and Ming dynasties and was probably manufactured in Kwangtung province. There are two principal types: yellowish or brown jars ornamented with dragon patterns, made probably from the thirteenth to the fifteenth centuries; and blue or green pieces, undecorated, of the fourteenth to sixteenth centuries. Both are a hard glazed ware, similar to Chinese household vessels, of no great value in that country, and were probably specially manufactured for export to Malaysia, where distance and rarity enhanced the price enormously. The natives seem to have felt themselves totally unable to imitate these pieces, and made no attempts to do so.

The pottery which the Japanese obtained in the Philippines in the sixteenth and seventeenth centuries and still call Luzon ware, is of a different type. It is not known whether it represents a third variety of Chinese importation, of which the Japanese demand has drained the islands; or an import from Siam, similarly dissipated; or a manufacture in Luzon by Chinese immigrants.

Burial jars, some of native and others of Chinese origin, have been found in the Batanes and Babuyanes islands north of Luzon, on Mindoro, and in western Mindanao. Interment in pottery vessels must thus have once been widely diffused in the Philippines, as it was in Borneo.

Boats. All the coastwise Filipinos used boats of the well known East Indian and Oceanic type—the outrigger vessel. Some, which were really ships, carried a hundred rowers and thirty fighting men.

Fig. 18.   Moro Outrigger Canoes

They were of course built up of planks, while smaller examples were dug out of a log. All but the smallest canoes were provided with two outriggers—stout bamboos or light logs extending parallel with the hull but held at some distance from it by a bamboo framework. The outriggers made the boat practically impossible to overturn. Even a vessel entirely filled with water could not capsize, nor, being built wholly of floatable materials, could it sink. Wooden pegs and rattan lashings held the parts together. On the larger war vessels, a platform raised above the middle length of the hull served the fighters; and these in turn were protected by an awning of mats. The mast, or sometimes two, could be shipped or lowered with the sail, which in former times was probably of matting. Paddles were also used for propulsion. The draft was very shallow, allowing even the larger boats to be drawn up on shore over night or on occasion. With such vessels the Moros long practised piracy and contested control of the southern seas with the Spaniards. A complete boat of this type, though smaller than the war *praos,* is exhibited in the collection.

Fire-Making. The Filipinos, like most natives that possess bamboo, did not employ the firedrill, which is most practical in wood, but used the firesaw to produce combustion by friction. This saw consists of a bamboo edge rubbed back and forth in a notch in a horizontal piece. The siliceous particles contained in the bamboo increase friction and usually ensure the prompt production of a spark.

Another method, seemingly restricted to Palawan, is to draw a rattan cord through a notch cut on the under side of a stick or slab of bamboo held down with the foot. This plan allows the full lift of the back to be applied as the operator stands, and is very effective.   Another advantage is that the cord can be carried about coiled into an armlet.

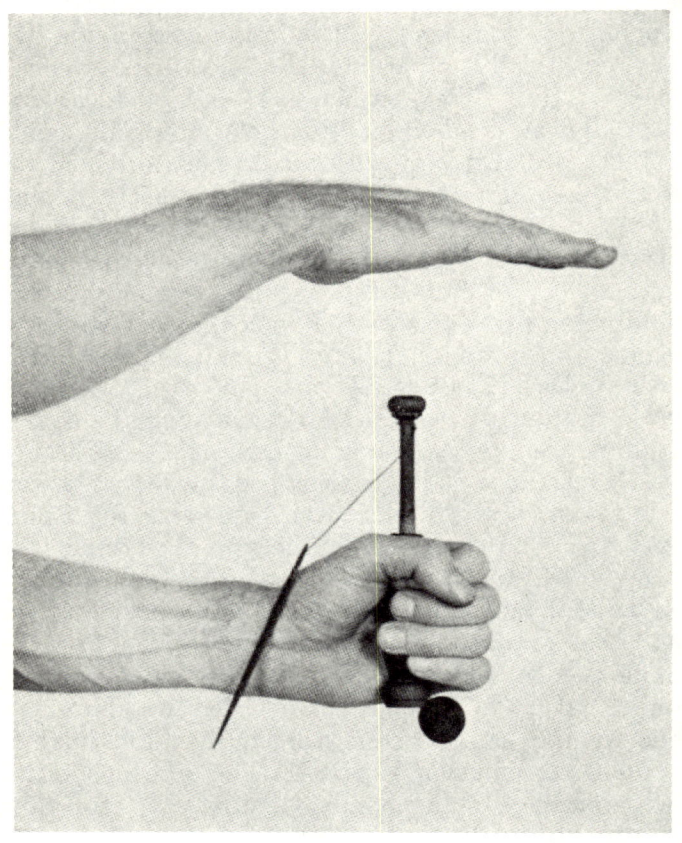

Fig. 19.   Use of the Fire Piston producing a Spark by Sudden Air Compression.

The fire piston is an extremely interesting device employed by some of the Tinggian of Luzon and the Bukidnon of Mindanao.   A plunger works snugly in a wood, bamboo, horn, or metal tube.   A little tinder is laid inside. A smart blow on the knob heading the plunger compresses the air to the point of producing heat enough to ignite the cotton; but considerable dexterity is required for success. The origin of this device remains obscure. It seems hardly capable of designed invention by any but a civilized people conversant with physical laws; and no analogous implement is certainly known which could have led to the discovery by accident. The cannon is perhaps the most likely prototype whose suggestion led to the uncalculated invention; but the blowgun, the smith's bellows, and the betel mortar also present similarities. The fire piston occurs also in Borneo, Java, Sumatra, Molucca—in fact wherever the true Malay has established himself; and in Burma, Siam, and Anam. Its employment in the Philippines precisely by the uncultivated tribes in the interior, the "Indonesians" or Proto-Malays, is therefore puzzling, and another of the many indications of the intricacy of Filipino civilization. The fire piston has also been known in Europe, but only as a sort of mechanical toy, and seems not to have been discovered there until the nineteenth century, so that its diffusion from this source over the whole of Indo-China and the East Indies within a generation or two, not to mention its firm establishment among the remote mountain Filipinos, seems incredible. The complete fascinating story of this extraordinary implement may never be recovered.

Flint and steel were perhaps the commonest fire implement in the Philippines, at least until the introduction of phosphorus matches, as might be expected from an iron-working people. If no other steel was available, the back of the bolo or head ax was used.

Iron Industry. All the peoples in the Philippines use iron, and no clear traces of a distinctive age of stone or copper have been found. Even the Negritos, although they do not work metal, may be said to be living in an iron age condition, because they possess knives obtained in trade from their neighbors.

There is every possibility that the islands may have been occupied before metals were known. This would be the period or condition of culture corresponding to the stone age of many other parts of the world. The reasons why no definite evidences of such a primitive type of culture have been found in the Philippines may be several. There has been very little archæological exploration. The natural density of vegetation would tend to conceal such remains as there might be. And finally, conditions in a typically tropical environment are not such as to favor the development of a distinctive stone culture. Bamboo, for instance, yields fairly serviceable spears, knives, and scrapers with but little shaping. It probably requires less technical skill to work into useful implements than stone. It is true that stone might well be employed to fashion the bamboo in such a nascent culture stage; but if so, a split cobble, made on occasion and immediately discarded, would easily answer all requirements, and thus come to leave no traces, or but the slightest, of the use of stone. At any rate, the traces have not been found; and so far back as our knowledge extends, all Philippine tribes have enjoyed the use of at least some metal tools, either of their own or of foreign manufacture.

A division can however be made between the native peoples having so little iron that it was mainly their utensil-making tools which were of that material, and the more advanced groups that possessed a greater abundance of the metal. In the former class there belong at the present time, besides the Negritos, some of the more remote pagans. Many of the unconverted nationalities, however, have long since not only obtained the material, but learned to work it: the Tinggian, the Kalinga, the Bontok, the Bagobo, and the Mandaya, all pagans, are smiths. At the time of discovery the majority of Philippine nations were in this condition. They knew how to work the metal, but did not yet obtain a sufficient supply to meet all their wants; so that iron and bamboo-tipped spears, for instance, were used side by side.

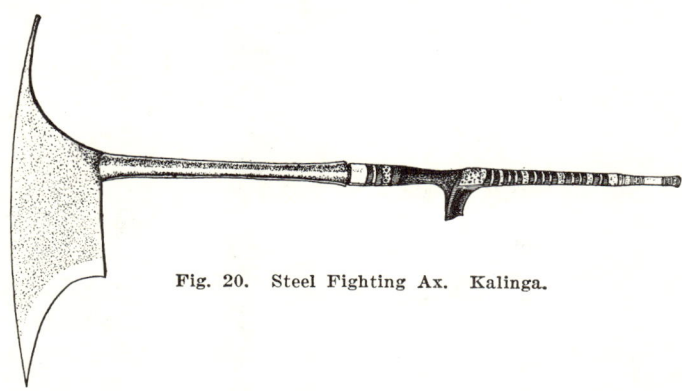

Fig. 20.   Steel Fighting Ax.   Kalinga.

This condition was the consequence of the iron industry not being native to the Philippines. It obviously reached them, probably by way of Borneo, from peoples among whom the art was already well developed. At first, manufactured articles are likely to have been introduced; subsequently, the raw material was imported in trade, and with it the

Fig. 21. Ifugao Bolo or Work and Fighting Knife, with Sheath and Belt

116

knowledge of working it. The operations of mining and smelting were not understood. In fact, very little advancement has been made in this direction through the past four centuries, possibly because the islands seem to be naturally poor in iron ores. The mineral has been worked in Bulacan, but the mining here appears to be entirely post-Spanish. In Borneo, on the other hand, even the interior tribes mine and smelt iron ore, so that the industry is likely to have a considerable antiquity. The Filipino smith always remained dependent on importation of his raw material, and in this sense his entire industry may be described as a parasitic one.

The plan of working is much the same among all the mountain tribes, and was no doubt followed in very similar form by the ancient Tagalog and Bisaya. The bar or ingot of metal is heated in a charcoal fire into which air is pumped from a bellows working in two or four bamboo cylinders. It is beaten with stone hammers, and the art of tempering by plunging into water is understood. In this way are made swords or battle axes, knives, the points or edges of agricultural implements, and the like. Contrary to the custom of Africa, where a similar iron technique prevails, the metal is scarcely used for ornaments in the Philippines, in all likelihood because the trade that brought in the raw material also introduced brass. The African not only works his iron, but extracts it, so that his industry, whatever its origin, is long since a self-sufficient home institution.

The fine steel blades, often chased or inlaid with other metals, which are so conspicuous in ethnological collections from the Philippines, are almost wholly the work of the Moros; in fact in part prob-

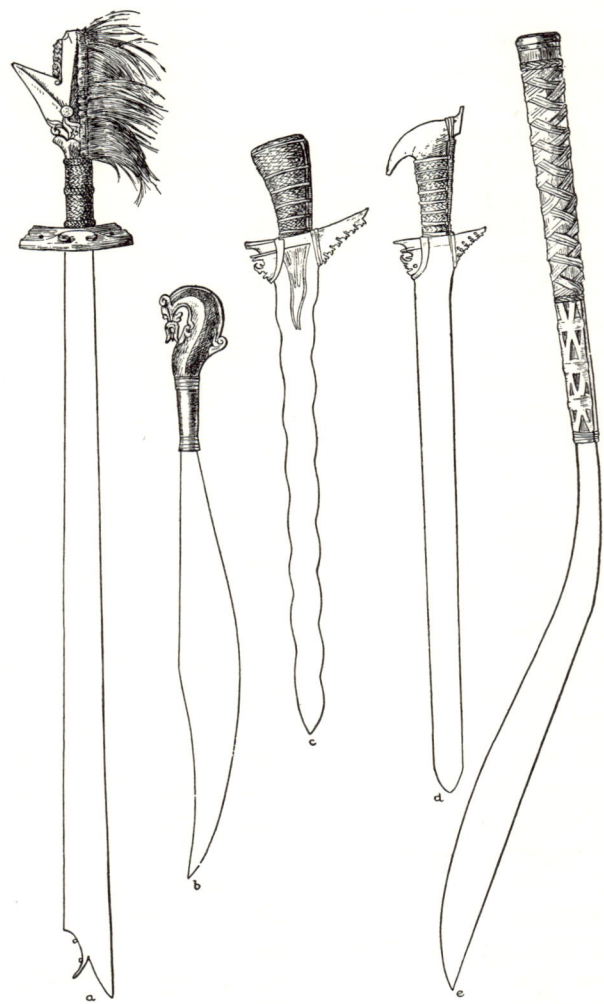

Fig. 22. Swords of the Mohammedans: *a, kampilan; b, barong; c, d,* wavy and straight *kris; e,* " beheading knife."

ably of non-Filipino Mohammedans in the islands farther west. Such weapons as the pagan tribes possess in this excellent workmanship—for instance, the Bagobo—are obtained from the Moros, or are made in inferior imitation of them. This is corroborated by the fact that in Luzon, and in fact all the islands other than Mindanao, the characteristic shapes as well as quality of Moro steel work are lacking.

There are several types of these beautiful blades: the *kris,* which comes both straight and wavy; the *kampilan,* a long straight sword; a bent blade of about the same length, for two-handed use—the "beheading knife"; and the *barong,* a heavy and rather short sword or knife with slightly curved edge. All these are cutting rather than thrusting weapons. The handles are of wood, horn, ivory, or brass, usually carved, and often exquisitely designed and executed. These types of weapons belong to the later stratum of East Indian culture of predominant Hindu and Arabic influence. They are in no sense peculiar to the Philippines; in fact, characteristic rather of Malacca and Java and Borneo, and unknown in the greater part of our archipelago.

The central and northern tribes chiefly use the *bolo,* a combination of weapon and tool, very similar to the *machete,* unornamented, long for a knife and somewhat short for a sword.

Copper, Bronze, and Gold. Brass and bronze represent a second set of trade materials whose import into the Philippines has been going on for a long time. All the tribes once used gongs manufactured in China, or at least made of Chinese bronze. These are still employed as the chief musical instrument by the Mohammedan as well as pagan tribes;

in fact, form the characteristic accompaniment to dances. As might be expected in view of their remote source, their value in native estimation is usually quite disproportionately high. It is customary to treasure them almost as heirlooms, and they frequently form part of the purchase price in transactions where dignity is an essential factor, especially weddings and the payment of blood money. Naturally, they were traded from tribe to tribe, so that even the interior peoples have long possessed a supply of them. Even the name by which these gongs are known, *gansa* or *agong,* is the same in origin as Javanese *gong* from which we derive our word.

Brass, that is zinc alloy, as opposed to the tin-copper mixture which makes bronze, is chiefly worked in the Mohammedan districts. However, there has been some permeation of more remote regions by the art of working this material, for the Bontok and other mountaineers of Luzon make

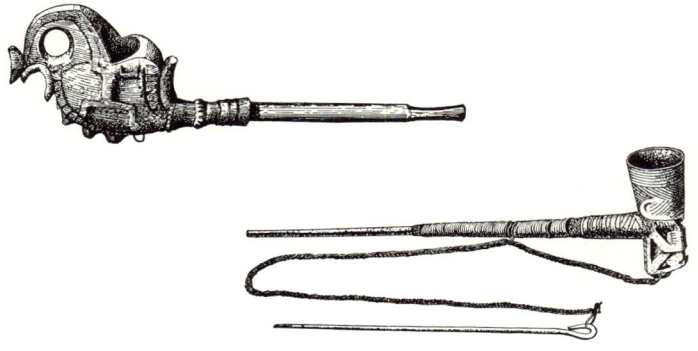

Fig. 23.   Pipes of Pottery—Nabaloi—and Cast Brass—Bontok

small castings in this metal although their product cannot compare in fineness with that of the Moros or even the pagan tribes adjacent to the Moros.

The process seems everywhere to be essentially the same. A model of the desired object is made in beeswax. This is surrounded by a clay mould. On heating, the wax melts and runs off, the molten brass

Fig. 24. Moro Betel Boxes Cast in Brass. The lower is inlaid with soft white metal.

or sometimes copper is then poured in its place, and the clay mould broken away. This is what is technically known as the *cire perdue* process. The Bontok chiefly cast small pipes in this way. The Mohammedans make belts, anklets, bracelets, sword handles, blades, bells, and boxes for betel. These betel boxes usually contain compartments, and are sometimes inlaid with designs in softer metal. The entire art is clearly of Asiatic origin and even its simpler forms must be looked upon as local degenerations and not as truly native industries. The brass is always imported.

The one metal which the Filipino can possibly lay claim to have discovered the use and working of, is gold. This occurs in many of the islands, in fact on all the larger ones; never in great quantity, but sufficient to repay its extraction by a people whose labor possesses no great economic value. The gold was obtained both in placers and in bed rock. Northern Luzon was apparently the source of greatest supply, and when the Spaniards occupied the coast districts, they found the so-called Igorot in the habit of descending from the mountains to exchange gold for the products and imported trade articles of the lowlanders. In the region of Suyok in Lepanto, the Kankanai still mine some gold in this way. They use stone hammers for the purpose. Elsewhere in the islands gold is sometimes washed out of the river gravels; but this is among Christianized peoples. Ornaments of gold were also found in use among all the tribes by the Spaniards, and continue to be prized and worn by some of them.

This development of the gold industry by no means argues a similar proficiency of the Filipino in the use of other metals. Gold usually occurs in the pure metallic state, and its softness renders it very easy to work by beating between stones. Neither smelting nor casting is necessary. In a sense, therefore, the gold industry as the Filipinos know it is not properly a metallurgical art.

It would be interesting to know whether the natives themselves discovered the presence of gold in their country and the fact that it could be worked into ornaments, or whether they became aware of its possibilities only after the knowledge of other metals had reached them from outside and stimulated them to the acquisition of gold.

Fig. 25. Brass Vase. Moro.

Baskets and Mats. Without exception, every nationality in the Philippines makes baskets. The types of vessels and the techniques employed are curiously uniform. Of course, there occur local

Fig. 26. Philippine Baskets. Checker or wicker weave: *b*, Hill people of Panay; *c*, Bontok. Twilled: *a*, Tagalog; *e*, Tirurai. Single-rod coiled: *d*, Bagobo; *f*, Bontok.

differences of shape and pattern; but the superficiality of these variations is much more conspicuous than their distinctness.

The simplest process in which baskets are made is the ordinary "in and out" or cloth weave. This is used by every Filipino tribe, not only for baskets but for matting. This technique is usually designated wicker or checker ware.

When this weave is slightly elaborated through each strand or splint being passed over and under two or more transverse strands at a time, instead of over and under only one, a diagonal effect can be obtained which easily yields patterns if materials of two colors are employed. This process is twilling, and is equally adaptable to baskets and to mats. It is by far the most commonly used weave throughout the Philippines. Its predominance is rather common in tropical countries, and seems to be the outcome of the qualities of the materials provided by nature. Bamboo, rattan, palm leaves, and other materials that split easily into thin flat strips or splints render work in twilling rapid, and thus offer every inducement to the weaver to give this process the preference over others.

The third process used in Philippine basketry manufacture is that known as coiling. This is really a form of sewing, although usually performed without a needle. A foundation is coiled on itself and the successive layers are sewn or lashed together by more flexible wrappings. This process has been found in use in a variety of Philippine islands; so that while it may not enjoy a universal distribution, it is clearly quite generally diffused. Technically, two chief types of coiling are distinguished: single and multiple rod. In the latter a bundle of stems replaces the single rod foundation of the former. The world over, multiple foundation is probably the more common. It is therefore rather strange that not a single basket coiled on a multiple foundation seems to have been reported from the Philippines. Possibly the preference of the islanders for the unit foundation is to be explained by their having materials available which easily come in considerable lengths and split into strips of uniform thickness. Where round twigs have to be used as foundation in coiling, considerable paring or other preparation is normally necessary to overcome their natural taper; which if uncorrected would render the finished basket coarse in texture and irregular in form. The unevenness in such case is much more easily overcome by operating with three or more rods treated as a bundle. The luxuriant growths of monocotyledonous plants that flourish in the home of the Filipino perhaps have encouraged his predilection for the technique of unit foundation coiling. As might be expected, this predominance is not confined to the Philippines, but extends over adjacent parts of the world.

Twining, the process by which two or more weft strands are simultaneously wound among the warp, is one of the most widely spread of all basketry techniques, particularly in temperate latitudes, but is practically unknown in the Philippines. The entire collection of the Museum contains only one or two specimens made in this technique.

Matting of both the checker and twilled types is widely manufactured, but does not attain either the fineness or the great variety of uses as in some other parts of Oceania. Many of the mats are woven without any pattern. They rarely possess sufficient

Fig. 27. Tinggian Women Weaving.

127

softness to make possible their use as clothing. They are also not employed for house walls or as currency, as in certain Pacific islands.

Woven Textiles. From mats to cloth is only a step. Cloth, in fact, is merely matting made of thread-like material handled on a frame or loom. The two principal cloth materials of the ancient Filipino were cotton and *abacá,* the fiber of the banana-like plant known in commerce as Manila hemp. The cultivation of both of these has already been discussed under agriculture. Today, the use of cotton tends to prevail among the Christian and Mohammedan nationalities, that of *abacá* among the pagans of Mindanao. The *abacá* cloth is stiff and somewhat coarse but very durable, and lends itself to pleasing sombre shades of dye. In the Bontok region, old style cloth was woven chiefly of bark fibers.

The only weaving machinery known to the native was the hand loom, one end of which was suspended, while the other was frequently attached around the weaver's waist. As might be expected from such a habit, the bolt of cloth was often of some length, but rather narrow.

The Bagobo and Ifugao practise tie-dyeing. Bundles of fibers or threads are wrapped and then immersed. The wrapped portions preserve the natural color, the intervening spaces taking the dye. Very effective although rather difficult weaves are obtained by this process. The Bagobo also tie finished cloth into wrapped knots to produce patterns by dipping. Tie-dyeing has its highest development in India and among peoples influenced by India; but it also occurs in simple form as far out in the Pacific as Melanesia.

The very beautiful and often extremely valuable *piña* cloth of the Christian Filipino has already been mentioned. *Jusi* is woven of raw and prepared silk. The latter material is of course imported, or at least the art was. Linen, true hemp, and wool were also unknown to the Filipino prior to the arrival of Europeans.

Tapa, or bark cloth, although not a textile, is in its use a substitute for woven cloths, and is part of the ancient cultural property which the Filipinos share with the East Indians and Oceanians in general. It is made from the *balete* and other trees of the genera *Ficus* and *Artocarpus*. The inner bark is stripped off in layers, soaked, and beaten. Philippine bark cloth is rather hastily made and never attains either the fineness of texture or degree of ornamentation which distinguishes Polynesian tapa. It is rarely pounded into a pulp, but has its fibers remaining distinct; and whatever softness the material possesses is due rather to its natural qualities than to the preparation. This cloth of bark is the only one used by the Negritos, except for such true textiles as they may acquire in trade or plunder. It is also still to be found among a number of pagan tribes other than the Negritos, as appears from an inspection of the Museum's exhibit. It may have been used even by the ancient Tagalog and Bisaya.

Men's Clothing. The basic article of men's dress in the Philippines is the breechclout, popularly known among Americans as the G-string—a narrow strip of cloth passed between the legs and held up at each end by a belt. Sometimes the strip is long enough to serve both as belt and clout proper. The mountain tribes still adhere to the breechclout, and it was once universal among the brown peoples of

Fig. 28. Bagobo Dance, showing Dress and Weapons of Pagan Tribes influenced by Mohammedans.

130

the islands. The majority have now discarded it, but only because of the substitution of more elaborate dress. As for the aboriginal habits of the Negrito, there is some doubt. Today, he wears a clout of cloth when he can afford to trade it from his more advanced neighbors. If he cannot, he appears to be nearly equally content with a clout of bark cloth or nothing at all. It is therefore not unlikely that his ancient habit was complete nudity.

The first piece of clothing to be added to the breechclout was evidently a coat or jacket. This was usually short-sleeved, often sewn together in front, was put on over the head like a shirt, and was always collarless. The Spaniards found both Tagalog and Bisaya wearing these little coats. The Moros use them universally, and appear to have done so throughout the historic period. From them the Bagobo and other pagan tribes of the south have derived the custom. As usual, northern Luzon has remained more backward. Among the Tinggian, Kalinga, and Apayao, the jacket is worn, but among other mountain tribes it is rather rarely put on and some groups continue to do altogether without it. This article of clothing is thus clearly not aboriginally primitive on the one hand, nor very recent on the other. Its introduction into the islands appears to be pre-Mohammedan; and, like so many other things in Filipino civilization, its original source is almost certainly to be looked for on the mainland of Asia and therefore probably in India.

The third piece of dress which the Filipino put on in his history, was his trousers. Like the jacket or any tailored garments, trousers were of course adopted only after true cloth was in general use. Bark cloth is unsuitable, and skins the Filipino scarcely used. The trousers were usually short, both in the waist and the leg. Knee length was the most customary.

Trousers are likely to have been a Mohammedan introduction. The Bagobo and other pagans of Mindanao quite obviously wear them as a result of contact with the Moros. The Bisaya and Tagalog were still using the breechclout when the Spaniards first saw them. The pagans of Luzon do not wear breeches today, except so far as they have sporadically taken them up in imitation of the Christians, who in turn cut their trousers on the European model. The pre-Christian center of distribution of this garment is therefore clearly the Mohammedan region.

Shoes are very little worn by any of the natives even at the present time. In the old days, every variety of footwear seems to have been wholly unknown.

Headwear. As in so many other parts of the world, the head, as the most conspicuous part of the body, was adorned long before there was thought of protecting the feet. At present, the hat is perhaps the most striking article of wear throughout the archipelago. Other than the Mohammedan, who clings to the turban style of headdress, and a few of his neighbors, there is scarcely a brown people in the islands that does not habitually affect something that may properly be called a hat. With the tribes of Igorot affiliation, this is quite rudimentary: a basket about four inches in diameter, or even a wooden bowl, worn on the back instead of the top of the head, and serving either wholly as ornament or as a receptacle in which useful little things are carried. Those of the northern pagans who border

on Christian peoples wear hats that shield from sun
and rain; and the Christians put on a great variety.
These always differ as between one nationality and
another, and often several types are in use among
the same people.   They are made of basketry, palm
leaves, gourds, or wood.   Some are fully as large as
a parasol, but nearly flat.   Others are rounded and
attain considerable height.   The simpler forms
show only a single curvature; but in many parts
there is a definite distinction between crown and
brim.   There appear to be considerably more than
a hundred hat types worn in the archipelago, and
their thorough classification promises to be of great
interest.   There is perhaps no other manufactured
article whose distribution is so universal, and in
whose making fancy and style are accorded so large
a range.

At the same time, it is possible that this entire development has taken place in less than four hundred
years.   The first Spaniards described nothing that
might properly be called a hat, but had much to say
about kerchiefs or head cloths, usually called by their
Tagalog name, *potong*.   This appears to have been
a band or fillet of some width which was wound
around the head.   Among the Bisaya, wealthy men
sometimes edged them with gold.   Ruder tribes who
wore no *potong* dispensed wholly with head covering.   This head cloth was a convenient way of con-
spicuously distinguishing the brave.   The red *potong* was put on only if one had killed a man.   Embroidered borders are said to have been added after
the warrior had slain seven human beings, and long
loose cords or fringes were reserved for the specially valiant.   The Sambal are said to have worn
a special head cloth as a sign of mourning until they

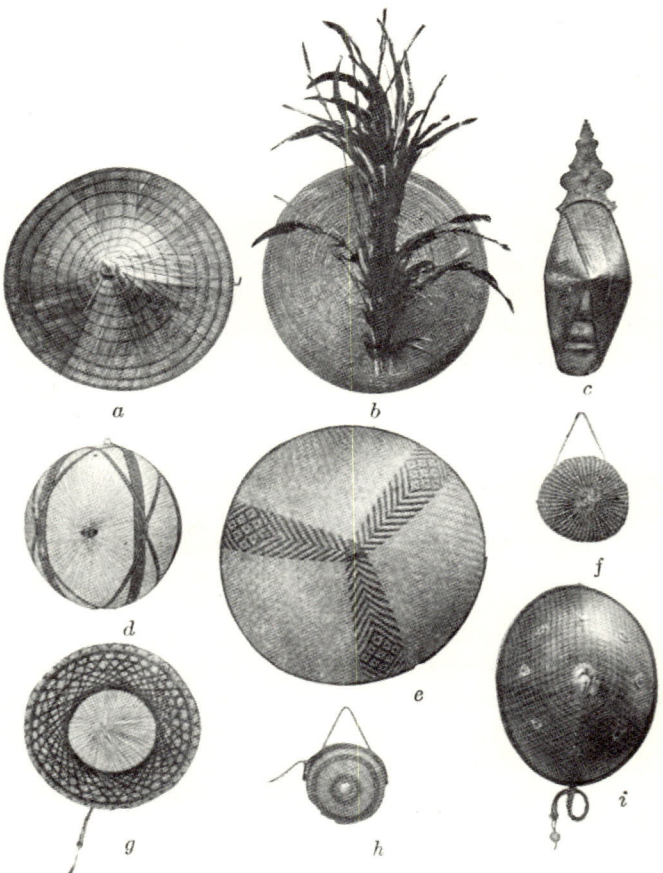

Fig. 29. Filipino Hats. *a*, Moro; *b*, Tirurai; *c*, Mandaya; *d*, Ilokano; *e*, Bikol; *f*, Bontok; *g*, Bisayan of Samar; *h*, Tinggian; *i*, Pampanga.

released themselves by killing a foe or stranger, much as the Bisaya cut their hair and ate no rice or cooked food after the death of a relative until they had obtained a similar absolution. The pagans of Mindanao follow analogous customs today: in place of the *potong*, they use a square kerchief, but among nearly all of them only he may wear a cloth dyed in a certain shade of red who has taken the necessary number of lives.

This, then, is the native headdress which the hat has tended to replace as Christianity prevailed and the old customs of killing and head-hunting fell into disuse as social insignia. Under this view, the small hats of the interior tribes of Luzon become very interesting. Some of these groups remained wholly without contact with the Spaniards or at least sufficiently aloof to take nothing over from them directly. Their miniature hats accordingly would seem to represent a development of their own customs; which, however, may have occurred only after they had received the necessary stimulus through the example of their more affected neighbors.

As to the head cloth, it is somewhat difficult to form a just historic appraisal. Mohammedanism is at once suggested. It is however entirely possible that the usage antedates the introduction of this faith. The connection of the head cloth with martial prowess is of course not Mohammedan, but typically Malaysian. Customs of this type are in fact so deeply ingrained in the aboriginal culture of the East Indies that one would be inclined to look for a considerably greater antiquity of the *potong* than the period of the first introduction of Mohammedanism would cover. All that can be said to the contrary is that, if the hat in little more than three hundred years came to be adopted almost universally without being associated with any such deeply

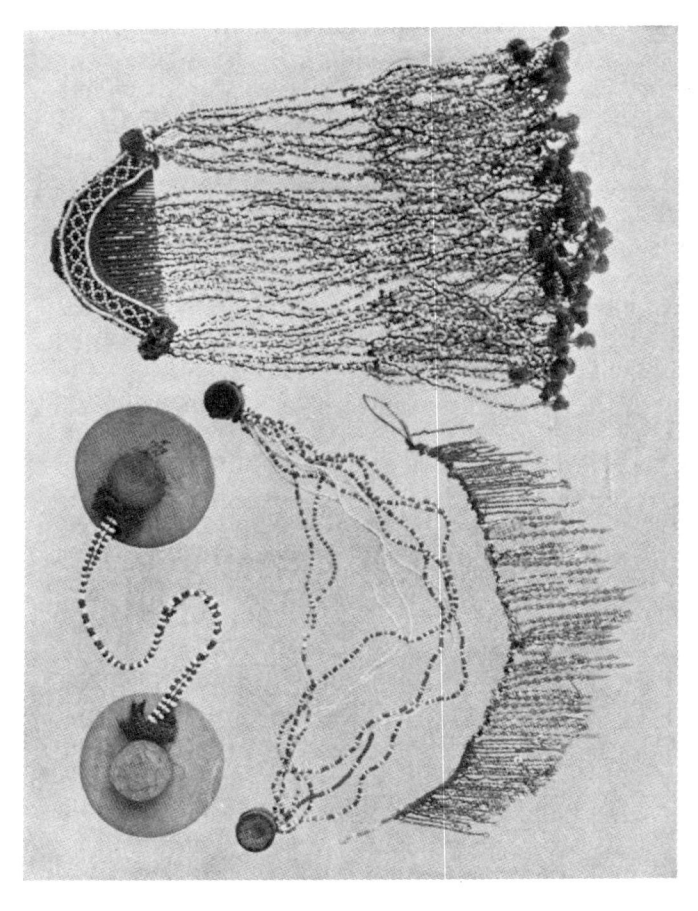

Fig. 30. Bagobo Ear Ornaments of Shell and Bead-Fringed Comb worn as a Hair Orname

136

rooted institution as head-hunting, it is conceivable that two centuries might have sufficed for the majority of tribes to have taken over the idea of the head cloth from the Mohammedan and fit it into their existent practices by connecting it with ideas of warlike distinction. Fashion in the narrower sense of the term undoubtedly plays and varies much more slowly among rude and semi-civilized peoples than among ourselves; but this conservatism or lack of imagination is compensated for by a much greater readiness to adopt fundamental changes in dress, particularly where these involve only additions to what is already in use.

Women's Dress. For women, the fundamental dress in the Philippines is that which is prevalent not only throughout the East Indies, but in the warmer portions of Eastern Asia: the *sarong* or unsewn skirt. This is nothing but a piece of cloth wound several times about the waist, held up by having its upper edge tucked in, and falling to the knees, ankles, or somewhere between. This is still the woman's skirt wherever ancient usage is adhered to in the Philippines. Pagan tribes such as the Bagobo replace the *sarong* by the bag or tube-like skirt that is sewn together, and is seemingly the result of contact with either Christians or Mohammedans. This is a far less beautiful garment, among a people whose art of dressmaking remains unrefined, than the *sarong;* because the latter falls naturally into folds and is capable of innumerable niceties of adjustment and draping.

The Tagalog and Bisaya, as well as the Moro women at the time of discovery, had already added to the skirt a jacket quite similar to that of the men. It was in fact the same garment altered only in details. These ancient jackets appear to be well represented by those worn by Bagobo women today —possibly even to the elaborate shell bead decoration favored by the latter. The mountaineers of Luzon scarcely knew the article. The Nabaloi, Kankanai, Tinggian, Kalinga, and even Apayao and Ilongot women now wear it more or less regularly; but these tribes have maintained trade contacts with the Ilokano or other Christians, and the barebreasted Ifugao and Bontok more probably represent the ancient custom of all the interior tribes. The modern Christian Filipina has given up the jacket and in most cases the *sarong*. Her dress differs somewhat from that of European women, but is basically of the same type and derived from it.

Hair, Teeth, and Tattoo. The ancient Filipino man wore his hair long and his adherence to this custom is a very fair index of the degree of his civilization, or rather his subjugation to Christian influence. The unaffected pagan tribes still maintain the old practice. The Tagalog formerly let the hair flow to the shoulder, the Cagayan, like the neighboring Kalinga of today, allowed it to fall free as far as it would, and valued length as beauty. The Ilokano cut it somewhat; the Sambal shaved the front half of the head, but wore a great loose shock on the middle of the skull. A similar style is still adhered to by the Negrito Batak of Palawan. The Bisaya, according to some accounts, cut their hair somewhat shorter than any of the Luzon tribes; according to others, trimmed it in a sort of queue. Of the Mohammedans, the Yakan and Lanao Moros still wear their hair long.

For women, the usual style was to leave the hair unconfined. Here also there were national fashions.

Tagalog ladies, for instance, wound their hair in a knot.

The practice of tattooing has everywhere yielded before Christianity and Mohammedanism, but appears to have been nearly as general a custom as the habit of wearing the hair long, especially among the men; and is therefore a similar index of status of civilization. Tattooing is undoubtedly an ancient Malaysian institution. Like the head cloth, it tends to be used as a means of indicating prowess. It is however clear that tattooing, long hair, and headhunting tend very strongly to coexist and to go out of use together. Of the tribes now civilized, the Bisaya were the most given to tattooing, covering almost the entire body. So striking was their appearance, that for the first generation or two their customary name among the Spaniards was *Pintados*, "the painted ones." The Tagalog tattooed very much less. Of the Luzon tribes now civilized, the Ilokano seem to have been the most addicted to the practice, which agrees well with the strong hold which the custom still retains among the pagans adjacent to them. The tribes of Mindanao were less inclined to tattoo than the Bisaya, in spite of their geographical proximity to them; and today follow the custom sparingly. Mohammedan example is the probable cause.

The Negrito has already been mentioned as scarifying his body instead of tattooing it, because the natural pigment in his skin is sufficient to prevent any introduced coloring matter from being conspicuous.

The overwhelming majority of Philippine tribes agreed with their kinsmen of the East Indies in filing and blackening the teeth. The chief exception is furnished by most of the Negritos and the mountaineers of Luzon. These do not follow the practice today. It is therefore likely that the custom never reached them, which would indicate that it did not form part of the most ancient stratum of culture in the islands. It fits with this view that the pagans of Mindanao, who have been more subject to ancient outside influences in other respects, file their teeth, usually to points. Thirteenth century Chinese accounts speak of Negrito tribes with white teeth; which indicates that the more advanced coast dwellers were already blackening their teeth at that time. Both filing and blackening are at first extremely repellent to people not accustomed to the practice, but like other fashions are of course esteemed beautiful by the people who follow them.

CHAPTER IV

SOCIETY

THE basic plan of Filipino society is one that dispenses wholly with constituted authority. Men of course differ in influence according to wealth, bravery, and wisdom; and the station in life they acquire tends strongly to be passed on to their sons by inheritance, particularly so far as it rests on the important factor of property. Authority over other men, however, is not transmitted, because such authority does not exist. In short, the primitive Filipino lacks totally the concept of the state which is so fundamental in all our thought about social groups. This does not mean that the Filipino lacks a system of law; in fact, as shown in a following section, he possesses a rather elaborate law and lives up to its theoretical justice to about the same degree as do we. These may seem contradictory statements. But they are so only from the point of view of our own civilization, which derives law from the state; whereas it is clear from the history of human culture that definitely regulatory law codes are in general far more ancient than definitely organized states. In fact, it would seem that the Filipino's law is intricate and refined just in proportion as he has remained primitively non-political. His beginnings in the direction of state organization were made through the channel of kingship; and it is plain that autocracy, although it may coincide with law, can get along with a minimum thereof, whereas when every man is every man's equal, some generally accepted system of right and wrong must prevail or chaos ensues. The difference, then, between the primitive Filipino and ourselves is not at all in the respective absence and presence of law, nor even so much in his lesser development thereof, as in the fact that the channels through which his law operates are distinctly non-political.

The Barangay Community. The Filipino thus follows in his community life a social grouping which we have largely replaced by a political one. Wherever he has remained primitive, the structural basis of his society is either the family of blood relatives or the *barangay*. In the main, these two plans coincide. The *barangay* is a group of people living in one locality and following one leader; they are either his kinsmen, his slaves, or his economic dependents. The basis of this unit seems to be the kin group, subsequently expanded by the inclusion of those who voluntarily or involuntarily have come into more or less permanent relation with it. The *barangay* was the plan on which the majority of the coast dwellers who are now Christian were organized at the time of discovery.

In the mountains of Luzon, the *barangay* is not so clearly defined, but actual conditions are not very different. As direct slavery is little developed, all individuals in the community are nearly on a single level, adhering among one another largely in virtue of their degree of kinship. Inasmuch as relationship is reckoned equally in the male and female line, it is obvious that every person is a member, through his father and mother, of two kin groups; and of course of a larger number as he traces his descent farther back. If one of the several groups with which he is thus connected has its interests affected,

he immediately acts with it. When the occasion has
passed, he may the next time be called upon to join
another group. If two groups clash with which he
is about equally affiliated, he is likely to serve as
intermediary, to use every effort to bring about a
reconcilement, and in this way to preserve to a considerable extent cohesion within the community.
Within each group with which he thus from time to
time acts, there is a recognized leader; the head,
through his lifetime, of a family which theoretically
is perpetual. He is the head because of superior
competence; which in turn rests on distinguished
wealth or bravery. Courage itself and fighting ability are of course not always transmitted from father
to son, but wealth is; and inasmuch as the ability to
fight successfully depends very largely on the possession of property, the leadership within the family
group is quite normally directly hereditary. This
is the plan of society under which the Ifugao, the
Bontok, and to a greater or less degree all the pagans of Luzon live.

The *barangay* system looks very much like an
extension of the mountaineers' plan of society.
Wealth was probably more readily accumulated on
the coast and thus afforded greater opportunity for
its irregular distribution and concentration in relatively fewer hands. This, in turn, encouraged slavery, which throughout the Philippines has always
been largely the result of debt or economic causes.
In these ways leadership became more pronounced.
Once it became powerful enough for its recognition
to transcend the bonds of immediate kinship, and
was accepted over a district as such, no matter how
small, the *barangay* plan was in force; and in a
sense too, the beginnings of a political organization

had been laid. From the point of view of development, however, the step from the anarchic mountain system to that of the *barangay* was a very short one.

With all this first step, the lowland Filipino of three or four centuries ago had however reached only the germ of a political constitution of society. He never succeeded in welding the little local *barangays* into larger units. This was the reason the Spaniards succeeded so easily in subjugating the larger part of the islands with a force that at first sight must always seem inadequate. The head of each *barangay* acted for himself and his people with him. As an early observer puts it, each was intent on his own interests, even though they might be brothers. If one acquired supremacy, it was merely a manifestation of superior ferocity and capacity in combat, either in his own person or that of his following. In that case his overlordship was to an extent recognized; but passed away as soon as his power fell to pieces with his death or from any other cause. The ancient political history of the Philippines was accordingly one endless succession of insults, jealousies, threats, murders, feuds, and reconciliations between the innumerable little *barangays;* without any unifications or consolidations ever occurring except of the most superficial and transitory kind.

Indian civilization, probably because its source was remote and its transmission indirect, never affected Filipino society as it affected Filipino knowledge and thought; but yet it could scarcely have passed by without leaving some traces. The last and declining phase of this influence seems to have entered the Philippines chiefly from the south and to have carried with it, to as far as the Bisayan

Islands, the name and possibly some glimmerings of the idea of kingship. Magellan found the chieftains of Cebu bearing the Indian title of rajah. And yet, their power does not appear to have been much greater than that of the *barangay* lords in Luzon. Statecraft as an enduring product never interested the Hindu very much. His claim to a high place in the history of civilization rests on his achievements in religion, philosophy, and literature. With such a type of culture first filtered through other channels and then seeping into an almost unorganized native society, one should not expect much result in the way of political upbuilding.

Mohammedan Influences. With the Mohammedan it was different. From the time of the founder of his faith he has been accustomed to the idea of absolute rule on earth. So deeply ingrained is this crude but effective concept that it has always remained characteristic of Islam, and still keeps a powerful hold on its devotees. If the Hindu had introduced the name of kingship into the Philippines, the Mohammedan imported the fact. The Sultans of Sulu and of Magindanao definitely attempted to rule as autocrats over large districts; and in some measure they succeeded. Of course, their fortunes were variable, since in the very nature of autocracy the degree of absolutism exercised depends to a preponderating extent on the individuality of the ruler. Living at the peripheries of the Mohammedan world, and among people whom Islam had therefore affected less deeply than the majority of its converts, the Filipino sultans held somewhat less complete sway than many of their colleagues in other parts of the world. At least in plan, however, they held power by the same right and by the same means; and under them the various *datos* or local chiefs were in turn minor autocrats. There is no question that this scheme of political organization gave the Mohammedans a military efficiency on a much larger scale than the other Filipinos possessed and was the cause which enabled them to preserve their independence for three hundred years after these had succumbed. In fact, their power was not broken until steam gunboats drove their fleets of light sailing vessels from the sea: and even then the suzerainty of Spain remained rather shadowy to the end.

In deeper perspective, however, the fairly successful states achieved by the Mohammedans are characteristic of Mohammedan culture and not of the Filipino. They represent a late and brief phase in the history of the islands, a phase which always remained essentially alien and affected only one end of the archipelago.

The pagans of Mindanao did not wholly escape the influence of Mohammedanism, although they retained their independence and native religion. Over most of the interior of this island, the *dato* both exercises greater power and maintains it over a larger area, than the family head among the mountaineers of Luzon. Here, then, a comparatively recent change has taken place.

The conclusion is that the Bontok, Ifugao, and adjacent tribes represent the original type of political society that once prevailed over all the Philippines. While the other nationalities have more or less altered politically, the causes and sequences of the development are clear. These causes were, in minor degree, economic progress; and prevailingly, the importation or example of foreign institutions.

Social Classes. Under these alterations of political organization, Filipino society persisted with fundamental continuity and very little change. Everywhere three strata of society were recognized. Those of the Ifugao—the wealthy, middle class, and poor—have already been mentioned. The same classes were established among the other pagans of Luzon. They existed also among the nationalities now Christian, although here their coloring was somewhat different. With the Tagalog and Bisaya, for instance, the rich were called the rulers; rank nominally superseded wealth; but actually the concentration of wealth was what made rank.

The middle class had become the common people —in the language of the Spaniards, the plebeians. The poor were slaves, either by capture or through debt servitude. Among the pagans of today, economic obligations are transmitted undiminished from father to son. When the Tagalog converted such obligation into peonage, serfdom, and finally outright slavery, there was therefore no wrench to custom when slavery became heritable.

Throughout the lowlands two classes of slaves were recognized: those who were absolute property and served in their master's house; and those who maintained establishments and families of their own but were liable to constant service. Among the Tagalog, the former were known as *sagigilid,* "those at the margin," that is, at the fringe of society. The better situated slaves or *namamahay,* "those who live in their own house," possessed the right of compelling their master to free them on tendering to him their proper value, whereas the full slave might be manumitted by his owner, but could not exact his own release. The value of a slave was put at ten taels of gold, or about eighty Spanish pesos, of a *namamahay* about half—very considerable amounts in view of the high value of money at the time and in so remote a region. For the Tagalog it is expressly stated that slaves constituted "their greatest wealth and capital." That the institution of slavery was very deeply rooted among this people and the Bisaya, is shown by the fact that a slave might be divided between heirs. If the father was survived by two sons and but one slave, the latter served his two new masters alternately for equal periods. Somewhat similar was the arrangement which made the child of a slave and a free man a half slave who served his master for alternate moons. It is even stated that a child of such a half slave and a free person was reckoned a quarter slave.

In Mindanao, the individual actually exercising sovereignty, no matter over how small a district, is the *dato;* whereas his sons, younger brothers, and the collateral or lineal descendants of a former *dato* are *timawa.* Although not ruling, these are reckoned of the same nobility as the *dato.* The same system prevailed among the ancient Bisaya and Tagalog; except that here the term *timawa* was applied to the common mass of free people as opposed to slaves. The Bisaya named their ruling class *dato* and the Tagalog *maginoo.*

It is very evident from all this that one trait is and has been shared by all Filipinos, no matter what their general condition of civilization: society is classified into horizontal strata, differing in rank, honor, power, and due. The idea of lineage is very strongly developed, and even the most primitive native makes every effort to maintain the position in

the world which his fathers occupied and to trans-
mit it unimpaired to his descendants. This feeling
is intensified by the preservation of genealogies.
An Ifugao or Bontok that amounts to anything at
all can always recount his ancestors on the mother's
as well as the father's side for five or six generations back. Among the Christians this faculty has
perhaps become somewhat stunted, but before their
conversion peoples like the Tagalog and Bisaya
seem to have kept record of their family trees to an
even greater extent. In fact, writing was employed
by them chiefly for this purpose, the genealogies,
after a few generations, being embroidered with
fanciful legends and ultimately merged into more or
less mythical accounts and tales of the origin of the
world. The Spaniards who alluded to these traditions unfortunately have not preserved them, but
their type is familiar from Malaysia and Polynesia
generally. Among the Philippine Mohammedans
the same tendency persists, although the new religion has somewhat altered the form. The Moro
sultans have genealogies that go back to the creation
of the world, but the old native cosmogonies have
been replaced by lines of descent beginning with
Adam and passing through Noah, Abraham, and
Mohammed. The Moros preserve these genealogies, which are their only histories, in books written
in Arabic characters. These records are demonstrably accurate for a considerable number of generations back from the present, and at least approximately authentic over a period of about five
centuries.

While society is so incisively divided into ranks,
there is no trace in the Philippines of the principle
of clans or exogamic or totemic groups. These two

systems agree in being social classifications based on descent; they contrast in that clans are not in essence subordinated to one another in prestige or power but are regarded as equivalent units within the social fabric. It is true that references have occasionally been made which might seem construable as indicative of the existence of a clan scheme among some of the less advanced Filipinos. Thus the previously mentioned *ato* or small units within the Bontok towns might speculatively be construed as relics of a clan organization: but they are not exogamic, and persons may change their *ato* affiliation. The Ifugao have been said to be organized into "clans"; but again, the characteristic features of a true clan system—exogamy, the reckoning of descent exclusively in either the male or the female line, totemism—are all absent. Therefore, it is extremely likely that the Ifugao "clans" are only the familiar *barangay* or something similar. There is no objection to denominating such units clans, provided it is clearly realized that the groups are essentially the same as those existing among the other Filipinos, and of a thoroughly different kind from the Australian and American groups to which the word clan is usually applied.

Even if we had no farther evidence, it would be obvious from the general Filipino attitude as to kinship that the native could not well have developed a clan system without reconstituting his society. He reckons relationship and descent equally through the male and female lines: which plan and clan organization are in the nature of things mutually exclusive.

The Filipino, in these matters of social constitution, aligns himself with most the nations related to him throughout the East Indies, Polynesia, and Micronesia—in other words, those parts of Oceania inhabited by brown peoples.[1] In these regions the clan idea is little developed, and where it has taken root all has normally proved abortive. It is in the tracts inhabited by the black Australians, Papuans, and Melanesians, that there is found a luxuriance of the clan system, or vertical classification of society, as it might be called in distinction from the horizontal one of levels. And even among the blacks the concept of rank takes precedence in those very districts which are known to have been subjected to Malaysian or Polynesian influence, namely, the greater part of Melanesia and the coast of New Guinea. The generic plan of social institutions among the Filipinos is therefore evidently an old one, perhaps inherited jointly by them and the adjacent brown-skinned nations from the time of their original community.

The Sexes. The place of woman in Filipino society is a high one. Even where Islam has been accepted, she retains many of her old privileges, and the typical Mohammedan practices of seclusion, veiling, and subjection to her father or husband have made only little headway. Among all the pagans encountered by the Spaniards, or still remaining such, the native attitude may be defined as a complete freedom from any assumption that men and women differ in rank or otherwise than as nature provides in giving them different bodies. In short, the inevitable physiological differences are

1 Indo-China, both about Assam and in its eastern regions, frequently shows a clan system with matrilineal descent. On the islands, however, clear matrilinear reckoning has been found only in two, which lie close to the mainland of Asia: Sumatra and Formosa; with reports or possible traces in Borneo, Celebes, and Timor.

recognized, but they are not used as a starting point from which social distinctions or restrictions are developed as by so many other nations. The Filipino may well be described as an unconscious and thorough-going feminist.

Not only are descent and relationship reckoned equally through father and mother, or son and daughter, but the terms applied to kindred are normally identical. The Filipino says "uncle" as we do, whereas many or most nations of similar cultural level distinguish carefully between the father's brother and the mother's brother, as if a kinsman related to one through a woman must necessarily be a different kind of kinsman from him who is related through a male. Often, too, the corresponding relatives of different sex are included under a single term by the Filipino: *apo* is neither grandfather nor grandmother but grandparent; only when the sex is specifically to be emphasized are words for "man" and "woman" added.

The division of labor has none of the hardened rigidity which most uncivilized peoples observe. Men of course do the fighting, hunting, carpentering, and all violent work. They also sit in council or rule, as the case may be. But this simply means that women are normally less fitted by nature and disposition than men to engage in certain pursuits; and most other activities are indiscriminately followed by both sexes, or only more inclined to by one than the other. An American Indian would stamp himself as unmanly and ridiculous if he carried water, fetched wood, or cooked while he possessed any kinswomen; and his wife or daughter would feel and share in his disgrace. The Filipino takes turns with his wife tending the children and farming. If it is inconvenient for her to cook, he does so. He brings in the firewood. He does the heavier work of agriculture, while the more tedious occupations of transplanting and weeding rice generally fall to her. Often men and women go to their field labors together. Of course custom does considerably segregate the occupations of the sexes; but rarely to the point of enforcing the separation under penalty of stigma.

The "medium" who is the only priest or recognized religious officiator of the Filipino is, throughout the islands as a whole, as often a woman as a man. The Bisaya, Tagalog, Tinggian, and Subanun usually favored women for this office; men predominate among the Bontok, Ifugao, Bagobo, and Mandaya. No people excludes either sex.

Marriage. Marriage was universally by purchase, and a dwelling together by man and woman without the bride price having been formally paid over was illegitimate and cast a shadow on the children as well as the couple. The transaction must be looked upon as an expression of respect, of publicly professed value, and as ensuring a foundation for the economic and therefore social well being of the descendants of the couple. The woman is far from being bartered about like a pig. The first advances of courtship frequently come from her. At the wedding she acts in total equality with the groom. They sit on the same mat or eat out of one dish as the cardinal symbolic act of the rite.

Small children are often betrothed, especially among the well-to-do who lay stress on alliances suited to maintain family dignity. In any event there is always a formal function, sometimes two, which precede the wedding itself and may be con-

strued as official betrothals. Should either party
retract after these preliminaries, the other properly
regards itself as insulted and lodges a claim for
damages. The marriage act has a strong religious
coloring. Sacrifices are offered and prayers or
formulas recited to ensure the health, well being,
and harmony of the couple and their offspring.

Among the surviving pagans, those of Luzon, for
instance the Ifugao, conduct engagements and marriages with somewhat more elaborate formality, and
pay larger values for their brides, than the Bagobo
and other inhabitants of Mindanao; but the difference is only one of degree. The principles on which
marriage rests, and the nature of weddings, are
common to both groups of tribes; and everything
goes to show that the nationalities now Christian or
Mohammedan formerly followed customs of the
same type.

That the married woman's position is one of full
equality is clear from the fact that she enjoys thorough economic independence. She inherits property from her parents to the same degree as her
brothers or unmarried sisters, and passes it on to
her children without any claim upon it by her husband. He enjoys the use of her property, but only
as trustee for the children, and without the right of
selling it. Of course his own status corresponds.
All possessions acquired by either husband or wife
during marriage, other than through inheritance,
are community property, upon which only the children of the couple, and not the respective kinsmen
of each of them, have any claim. In case of divorce,
the community property is settled upon the children; if there are none, it is equally divided. It is

difficult to imagine an attitude of more complete non-discrimination between the sexes.

Under these conditions, marriage was naturally single: always in theory, and in most cases in practice. Even where, as among the Tagalog and Kalinga, the wealthy sometimes took several wives, one was reckoned the lawful spouse. The others were more or less recognized concubines, and their children of lower rank. Among tribes that strenuously maintain their personal independence, such as the Ifugao, an attempt by a husband to live with another woman normally leads to a compensatory claim against him, and often to divorce. Real polygamy was introduced only by the Mohammedans; and even the Moros in their actual practices still adhere rather closely to the generic Filipino spirit.

Divorce is easy and in no sense a disgrace. The dowry or bride price is returned, unless the husband is demonstrably at fault, in which case it is retained as compensation for the injury inflicted. Everything is restored as well as may be to the antenuptial status, and each party is free. Among many of the wild tribes most men and women change partners several times before settling down permanently with a congenial mate, and the ancient habit of the peoples now Christian seems to have been much the same. The Ifugao assess a fine called *hudhud* upon the spouse whose disposition or conduct is responsible for the dissolution of a marriage: this is in extinction of the mental anguish caused the innocent mate. A payment called *gibu* must be made by the widow before remarriage is permitted. Failure to pay the *gibu* would be an affront to the deceased wife or husband and her or his kin.

There is considerable tendency toward cousin marriage in the Philippines. The hero tales of the Tinggian are full of statements such as "It is good for us to be married because we are relatives," and even first cousins unite in wedlock. The modern Tinggian absolutely bar such unions, and regard the marriage of second cousins as somewhat scandalous. The Ifugao are allowed to break the prohibition against the marriage of second or third cousins by making a payment; the Subanun do the same between those of the first degree. The Bontok forbid only first cousins. The Bisaya always tried to procure a wife closely connected in relationship. The Tagalog insisted less on this point, but according to Father Chirino both nationalities permitted the marriage not only of first cousins but of uncle and niece, although Colin, a century later, while alluding to the fondness for marriage with remoter kin, specifies these degrees as prohibited. It would seem that the most primitive tribes were the most rigorous, and that with the growth of wealth and distinctions of rank the bars had been gradually let down in order to consolidate family property and prestige as much as possible. It is however rather significant that even the most backward Filipinos do not enforce the widely spread and absolute rule of many primitive peoples against wedlock with any person that is demonstrably akin.

There is nowhere any distinction, in these matters, between cross and parallel cousins, that is, the children of brother and sister as contrasted with the children of brother and brother or sister and sister. This is what might be expected from the fact that the Filipino looks upon his relatives through males and through females as identical. Only the Subanun say that if the son of a brother wishes to marry the daughter of a sister, he must pay a heavier fine than other cousins.

It may be added that restrictions on women before and after childbirth are of no great moment among the Filipinos, and even among the wilder tribes are as much hygienic in character as of the nature of taboos; and that adolescence ceremonies for girls— a distinctive feature of many primitive societies— have scarcely been reported.

The general high status of woman recurs among all the Malaysians as well as the Polynesians. It has suffered chiefly in proportion as Hindu, Mohammedan, and European influences have been operative. The mental attitude which it involves must therefore be regarded as an ancient and highly typical characteristic of the culture of the brown races of the Pacific, whereas the black peoples of Oceania —Australians, Papuans, and Melanesians—tend to draw a much sharper line between men and women, to the social disadvantage of the latter.

Law. Primitive Filipino law recognizes only relations between individuals and between groups of individuals united by blood, co-residence, or common interests. There are no offenses against the state, because there is no state. Every man is his own judge and executioner in all offenses committed against himself or his immediate group; but custom defines rather rigorously and sometimes intricately what his just rights and liabilities are.

In the case of the most serious offenses, such as killing and witchcraft, the only honorable recourse is to revenge, and he who did not attempt to attain it would brand himself as cowardly or meanspirited. All grievances not of the very first magnitude are however expected to be settled without violence. The injured party levies a fine upon the offender and utilizes every means of persuasion, appeal to a sense of justice, pressure, or threat to enforce its payment. The offender usually resists up to a certain point. To yield at once would be a confession of guilt, or at least an admission of weakness that might lead to future exactions. Sometimes counter claims are advanced, and usually the amount of liability is contested.

In minor cases the payment due may be settled in conference of the parties interested. Where the alleged offense is more serious, go-betweens are employed for a commission; or the community at large, that is its older and more influential men, gathers and renders a decision. Such a verdict, even if it cannot be enforced, puts the offender under the strain of resisting public sentiment. The Nabaloi have a recognized council of elders, the *tongtong,* which meets in such cases; and among the Tinggian the *lakay* or head man is prominent in the council. But the tribes farther removed from civilization and therefore presumably preserving in purer form the institutions of their ancestors—the Ifugao, for instance—settle all disputes without reference to anyone but the parties interested and their kinsmen or representatives. In Mindanao, where Mohammedan example has raised the head man to the fairly influential position of *dato* even among some of the pagans, justice is more largely dispensed by this individual; but this is obviously not the aboriginal usage. The Tagalog and other lowlanders were found by the Spaniards to be following much the same practice, the chieftain retaining for himself a considerable part of whatever fine was paid over. Still, even among these people, councils for the purpose of conducting trials are reported, so that it seems that the head man's power was probably less in native opinion and practice than it appeared to the Spaniards. The foreigner naturally tends to construe new institutions in terms of his own.

Laws of the Northern Pagans. Of course, the loose native system did not always result in full justice. The brave and the wealthy were in a position to exact undue penalties from the weak and the poor, and to whittle even equitable claims down to a fraction. The Ifugao frankly recognize that the fine due a well-to-do man, or due by him, is greater than that which a middle class or poor person receives or pays. The penalties exacted are about twice as great for each successive class. When the offender and injured party are of different classes, the fine is normally a compromise; thus, the poor are liable to the rich and the rich to the poor for about the amount which one middle class man would pay to the other for the same offense. Between people distantly related in blood, claims are pressed less strenuously and small compensation is accepted. Among very near relatives, even the most serious offenses are entirely condoned.

The first claim is of course normally against the actual offender, but his entire kin are ultimately liable in proportion to their degree of relationship. Where the criminal is one of the less influential persons of a group, the supposition is that he was acting at the instigation or at least with the cognizance of the head of the group, that is, its richest man; and the principal liability falls upon the latter. This supposition is probably well founded in the majority of cases. Thus the Ifugao distinguish between the *nungolat* or principal, "who was strong," the one who plans or directs the offense, whether or not he takes an active part in its commission; the *tombok,* or thrower, who actually hurls the weapon and who stands in the second degree of liability and likelihood of being attacked in revenge; third, the "companions of him who was strong," who merely assist or accompany the criminal; and fourth, the *montudol* or shower, who gives information facilitating the commission of the offense without otherwise participating. While kinsmen are always liable to a greater or less degree, merely on account of the intrinsic relation in which they stand to the offender, and irrespective of their degree of participation, husband and wife are not reckoned as kin among the Ifugao, and in fact may be parties to suits against each other.

Oaths are taken and witnesses heard, but when testimony is insufficient, recourse is had to ordeals, especially in minor cases, such as theft. Some form of trial by ordeal was at one time practised by every people in the Philippines and the pagans universally retain the institution. Almost invariably both parties were compelled to submit to the same test, such as plunging the hands into boiling water, handling or being touched with hot irons, and the like. In other cases, they threw eggs, sweet potatoes, or reed stalks at each other, the one hit being adjudged guilty. Sometimes the ordeal developed into a duel with lances. In other instances a wrestling match decided the issue, and so strong was the conviction of the innocent contender that he usually was the victor even over an opponent who was physically stronger.

The ordeals were always of a ceremonial nature and represent the same appeal from mundane to supernatural justice which characterized our own mediaeval ordeals. They possess a semi-civilized flavor rather out of keeping with the generally primitive attitude of the pagan Filipino. They are not practised in aboriginal America nor in certain outlying regions of the Old World, but prevail chiefly among those peoples of Europe, Africa, and Asia who are in the condition of culture that is sometimes described as barbarism. There is thus a considerable probability that the concept of the ordeal originated only once in the history of civilization at some point which cannot at present be determined, and spread from this center to those peoples of the three continents whose general level of civilization put them within range of accepting the institution. It seems rather likely that the ordeal was introduced into the Philippines as part of the same cultural movement which imported the institutions of animal sacrifice and augury.

Murder or assumed murder through sorcery are the most aggravated and perhaps the most frequent offenses with which native law deals. Intent is an important factor when life is lost. Witchcraft of course always implies intent. Pure accident without negligence imposes no liability in Ifugao eyes even if life is lost. Negligence without intent causes the imposition of a heavy fine. Where the killing is wilful, the Ifugao never accepts blood money, since this would stamp him as a person without honor. This is the general theory of all tribes: the debt of life must be paid in blood. But in more settled communities, there is a manifest inclination to facilitate the acceptance of property

settlements, especially after a feud threatens to go
on perpetually without marked advantage to either
side. Fine distinctions are sometimes made as to
carelessness and intent. An Ifugao, knowing that
his own life is being sought, may hurl a spear out
of his house in the direction of a noise that he hears
at night and slay a peaceful neighbor. Criminal
intent being lacking, he is not liable to the death
penalty; but negligence being obvious in that he
did not first make sure of the identity of his victim,
he is liable to a heavy fine.

The offense next in severity and perhaps in fre-
quency among the same people is adultery, for
which the penalty is also large. The bulk of the
fine goes to the offended spouse, the remainder to
his or her kin. The co-respondent is as fully liable
as the delinquent spouse: an injured wife, for instance, receives payment from both. A guilty man
is somewhat doubtfully subject to the death penalty
provided this is inflicted immediately by the aggrieved husband, who can then aver the justified
heat of passion.

Theft is a distinctly subordinate offense and less
frequent than denial or evasion of debts. In the
latter case, the aggrieved Ifugao is entitled to seize
an equivalent from the offender's property. He
must, however, do so openly, and if the owner is
absent leave behind him his bolo or some other article that will establish his identity. Should he fail
to do so, he himself is committing theft. In case the
thief or offender liable to a payment is distant and
cannot be reached, it is justifiable to appropriate the
amount of the claim from the property of any member of his community. The seizure is then held as
a pawn until its owner redeems it with the proper

fine, which he has exacted from his delinquent co-resident. Of course, this theory does not always work out, and sometimes leads to fresh litigation and conflicts; but it evidences a considerable sense of legal equity as well as a highly developed feeling for property.

The Filipino is extremely proud and sensitive, and his law protects him against moral and mental affronts even when no physical violence has been used and no property damaged. The Ifugao admits fines for slander, threats of violence, false accusation of crime, the employment of abusive or indecent language, and insults reflecting on honor, prestige, or rank. Among the tribes that accentuated differences in social standing and whose communities were presided over by a recognized chief, even heavier penalties attached to offenses of this character.

Codes of Other Tribes. The Subanun of Mindanao have theoretically accepted Mohammedan control of their justice, but have kept most of the provisions of their ancient law, so that it still rests essentially on the same foundation as the Ifugao code. The greatest difference is that the trials are formally conducted by the *dato* or a group of head men instead of go-betweens acting for the principals; and that one-half of the penalties paid go to the judge. Personal revenge being illegal, the life of offenders is rarely taken, even murder being condoned for by the *bangun* or blood money. Adultery brings a heavy fine, and even improper advances impose some liability. A husband is privileged to wound a wife on discovering her infidelity. Should he kill her, he is subject to fine. After the first outburst he is not allowed to do her any bodily injury.

For theft, the penalty is two or three times the value of the stolen article. Heavier fines attach to the rich than to the poor for the same offense. If a fine cannot be paid, the debtor becomes a temporary slave. He is not usually held longer than three years, except when the offense is adultery.

Among the ancient Pampanga, it was usual for communities to go to war if a chieftain or noble was slain. In time, however, such feuds were patched up, from seventy to one hundred taels of gold being paid for the original murder. One-half of this amount went to the bereaved children, the remainder to the kinsmen, less a commission to the chiefs of other communities or kin groups who effected the settlement. For the slaying of a common man by one of the nobility, the fine was ten to twenty taels, but in default of direct heirs of the victim, the amount was distributed largely among the nobility participating in the settlement. If a common man slew one of the nobility, he and his family were put to death. For murder among the common people, a fine was assessed, in default of which the offender was hanged or lanced. For the killing of a near kinsman, the death penalty was not inflicted. Theft required restitution plus a fine. A thief unable to pay was sold as a slave to another district. Arson of dwellings or crops was a serious offense which even members of the nobility must compensate for in full, whereas common people were executed, and their goods and if necessary their wives and children seized. "Insulting words caused great anger" and were considered a very grave offense. The culprits were fined in heavy sums "in order not to cause murders." Naturally, the common people might offend the nobility very much more poignantly than the latter had it in their power to violate the duller sensibilities of plebeians. When one chief insulted another, a decision was rendered by a still greater one, or by several of equal rank. If the offender was unwilling to submit to such judgment, he was at liberty to try to outdo his rival by lavishing greater expense on ceremonial festivals, he who succeeded in spending the larger sums being thereby accounted the more honorable.

The Moros of Magindanao and the Sulu possessed written codes translated into native dialects from old Arabic law. This law is Mohammedan in character, being based on the Koran and commentaries thereof, except for a few modifications in the direction of ancient native custom. No Hindu code seems ever to have reached the Philippines.

Economic Life. Property occupies a very large part of the Filipino's thought. This is manifest from the importance which it has in law as well as from its determining effect on social standing. Certainly the contrast is great between the Filipino and the American Indian who generally professed to hold property in light esteem and readily lavished it in opportunities of ostentatious liberality. In the Philippines, the attitude of the civilized and uncivilized peoples toward wealth is much the same. The latter are generally poorer, but if anything more attached to their possessions.

Since the economic practices of the Christian tribes have become somewhat altered in conformity with European standards, and those of the wild tribes of Mindanao and of the Negritos are very imperfectly known, the best picture of the native life in this aspect is preserved by the pagans of Luzon. The Ifugao distinguish two kinds of property:

purely personal belongings which can be disposed of at will, and second, property normally obtained by inheritance and therefore looked upon as being essentially owned by the family or lineage. This the individual holds much in the capacity of trustee. When such property is sold, a ceremonial known as *ibuy* must be made, and the agents and witnesses to the transfer receive commissions or at least presents definitely regulated by custom. One value of the *ibuy* obviously is that it makes a public record of the transfer.

The Ifugao is constantly going into debt. Sickness frequently makes necessary the purchase of animals required for the sacrifices which alone are believed capable of inducing recovery from illness. A death involves an elaborate feast for all who attend the funeral. Other occasions require expenditures which must be made from loans if available property is insufficient. The borrower often pledges a rice field or other valuables as collateral. Such a pawn is called *balal*. If a field is pledged, it can be held by the lender until full repayment is made; but it does not become his property even after two and three generations. Collateral is often repledged to another lender, and such procedure is regarded as legitimate, provided each succeeding loan is smaller than the first one. Death in no case extinguishes a debt.

Interest is known as *lupe* and is enormously high: the normal rate is one hundred percent for a year or any shorter period. A poor family running short of food may borrow rice a month before the harvest; they repay double the quantity a few weeks later. The debt doubles each succeeding year. Naturally, if the borrower does not soon pay off, he can

liquidate only by handing over a field or some other
article of considerable value. Frequently the *pa-
tang* is exacted—a partial advance payment of interest—almost a discount.

Every agent receives a fee whether his services be
rendered in a commercial transaction, the adjustment of a fine, or involve outright labor.

Rice fields are rented on a basis of one-half of the
crop to the landlord; he usually furnishes also one-
half of the seed, but this is repaid to him doubly
from the tenant's share. The latter performs all
labor and provides the animals for the sacrifices
needed to ensure a successful yield.

Rich men, not only among the Ifugao, but among
other mountain tribes, are expected at intervals to
give great festivals of a semi-religious character.
Besides being an occasion for feasting and merri-
ment, these are believed to contribute to the general
welfare of the community. Men of substance who
failed to make these ceremonies—at which great
quantities of animals are sacrificed and eaten—
would lose caste. The Ifugao call such ceremonies
honga and *uyauwe;* the Kankanai, *bumayas, mandit,*
and *begnas;* the Nabaloi, *pachit.*

Rice fields constitute the greatest single item of
Ifugao wealth and on the average make up probably nearly one-half of the property owned. Their
value runs from 250 to 800 pesos per acre, according
to locality. The holdings however are small. At
Kiangan about one family out of twelve possesses
no rice land whatever; only one-fifth own two acres
or more; and the total holdings of the wealthiest individual are twelve acres. When a field is sold,
nearly twice the stipulated price is actually paid, the
additions consisting in part of *lukbu* or fees to wit-

nesses and agents, and in part of gifts to the kin of the seller. The latter receive about one-half as much as the amount paid over to the owner, and the witnesses about one-quarter.

Similar economic conditions prevail among the Bontok. A field containing six thousand square feet is valued at two buffaloes or a hundred pesos. This is about seven hundred pesos per acre. If the field is rented, the landlord receives one-third of the crop. The gross yield, under his own cultivation, is about ten percent of the value of the field. The richest man in Bontok pueblo owns thirteen fields worth something over three thousand pesos. His personal property, consisting of buffaloes, pigs, stored rice, ornaments, and heirlooms, brings his total wealth to about ten thousand pesos. Wages are exceptionally low, averaging five centavos a day. As a fowl is worth ten times as much, and a pig averages perhaps eight pesos, it is obvious that even bare subsistence on the wage alone would be quite impossible. As a matter of fact, the laborer receives his food in addition to the wage.

The minuteness with which these head-hunting mountaineers value everything, even to immaterial possessions or privileges, is really remarkable. The appended list of Ifugao appraisals is representative. It is clear that the economic development of the native had far outstripped his technical, social, political, and intellectual progress.

While the valuations are here given in pesos or American half dollars, the actual basis of reckoning, both among the Bontok and the Ifugao, is the handful of rice in the stalk, the Spanish *manojo*. The Bontok call this *finge;* the Ifugao, *botek*. Its value among the latter is two and a half centavos, except during the half year immediately preceding the harvest, when it doubles. Small payments are frequently made in this rice currency; larger ones are figured in it or in pigs or buffaloes. The result of all of the many negotiations, sales, and loans is that even the primitive Filipino has acquired an unusual sense of numbers and great versatility in the use of figures. Arithmetical operations are however mental or performed with counters, and no system of numeral notation has been reported.

ECONOMIC VALUATIONS AMONG THE IFUGAO

	Pesos.
Rice fields with water rights, per acre	250–800
Sweet potato fields	no value
Coconut palm (without land)	5
Areca palm (without land)	.50
Slave	100
Buffalo	50–80
Pig	2.50–30
Fowl	.25–1
Commission for buying and bringing buffalo from Christian districts	10
Bronze gongs	8–250
Gold neck ornaments (intrinsic value of metal about one-sixth)	60–120
Strings of agate beads	250
Jars for rice wine	60–400
Damages varying according to wealth of the parties involved	
False Accusation	10–35
Curse ''may you die''	10–35
Adultery committed after preliminary marriage ceremony	5–20
after second ceremony	12–50
after final ceremony	25–100
with aggravation or insult (*hokwit*)	50–200
Wounding	80
plus cost of ceremonies for recovery and reconciliation	100

| Attempts to involve as an accomplice in a killing | 50–150 |
| Homicide, varied but little according to rank or wealth | 1000 |

Trade. As might be expected, trade is considerably developed. The pagan tribes do not transport very far; but articles that are sought after are frequently passed through a succession of groups. Manufactured articles as well as raw materials form the objects of this commerce. Frequently a particular industry is specialized at a given point, which then supplies a considerable district with its ware. Thus, in the region of Bontok, Samoki district makes and exports pottery; Baliwang, steel head-axes; Agawa, brass pipes; Sagada, cloth. In the same way, Barlig trades rattan, resin, and wax to other communities; Mayinit, salt; Tinglayan, tobacco; Suyok, gold. In these last cases natural supply is obviously the determining factor; but the localization of industries appears to be rather a matter of custom. This condition is so definitely stabilized as to lend a strangely civilized flavor to the industrial life of these otherwise so primitive tribes.

War. With all his gentleness of manner, the Filipino, like other East Indians, must be accounted a man of courage. He holds human life cheaply, and often his own as well as that of others. If his bravery on occasion melts into panic, such is the almost inevitable outcome of undisciplined combat. His failure over most of the islands to maintain his independence against the Spaniard is proof chiefly of the inefficiency of his political organization: the Moros, who as already mentioned were consolidated into kingdoms and subkingdoms instead of divided by innumerable feuds, thereby preserved their freedom much longer.

Fighting was a chronic act of Philippine society,

and the man lacking in personal courage enjoyed
but the slightest esteem, whatever his hereditary
station in life. But the endless conflicts scarcely
ever rose to the dignity of wars, because of inability
of the local groups to form themselves into larger
units. Among the tribes of the interior, even communities often failed to act as groups in a conflict,
and many of the combats were restricted to families.
This was particularly the case among groups like
the Ifugao who recognize no head men, and who,
when peaceable adjustment fails, have no recourse
but to take up arms. In such event, the contest is
likely to be confined to the kinsmen or immediate
adherents of those who have received or inflicted
the original injury. In the strict sense of the term,
then, warfare can scarcely be said to be practised
by the modern pagans, who rather alternate between
living in a state of peace and one of vendetta. To a
considerable extent this was also the condition of
the Christian tribes at the time of discovery.

Head-Hunting and the Debt of Life. The most
striking feature of this side of native life was the
practice of head-hunting, in which the less settled
Filipinos engaged with the same ardor as the tribes
of Borneo and the other East Indies. All through
Malaysia it appears to have been an immemorial
custom to decapitate the fallen foe and bring his
head home for triumphal display. A ritual celebra-
tion followed. Often, in fact, the feeling was strong
that an important ceremony could not be successfully conducted without at least one fresh head, and
a party would be organized to provide this requisite
for the proper carrying out of what religion or-
dained. Many tribes kept either the head or the
skull permanently hanging inside or before the

house. The Bontok buried, cleaned, and preserved the skull, and used the jaw as a gong handle. The more heads a warrior brought home, the greater was his renown, and the more influential his standing in the community. As civilization gradually advanced in Malaysia, and Indian and Arabic points of view came more and more to be adopted, the crudity of this primitive practice seems to have been recognized as unnecessary or even objectionable, and head-hunting as such fell into disuse. In religion, the custom of formal human sacrifice partially took its place; and as for a man's reputation, it was no longer felt necessary for him to display the physical proofs of his success in combat. The knowledge that he had slain so and so many enemies sufficed. But with all this comparative refinement of custom, the ancient attitude continued to be adhered to. The Javanese and Mohammedanized Malay have long ago ceased head-hunting; but the more primitive tribes, particularly of interior Borneo, still hold to the practice.

The same stages of development can be traced in the Philippines. All through northern Luzon, even along the coasts, the Spaniards found head-hunting in vogue. The Sambal, Ilokano, and Cagayan have long since given up the custom. The Tinggian and the Nabaloi have also discontinued the practice, but recollections of it remain in their traditions as well as in their ritual. The Apayao, Kalinga, Bontok, and Ifugao were still taking one another's heads with undiminished interest when the American appeared in the islands, and firm pressure was required to induce them to abandon the practice. In fact it is only in recent years that the custom has been generally stamped out; and in the remotest districts it is probably still followed when opportunity offers.

The Tagalog and Bisaya of old, like the modern Manobo, Mandaya, and Bagobo, and the Mohammedan groups, having come more fully under native civilizing influences, were no longer taking heads when the Spaniards came among them. Now and then they collected the ears of the dead or clipped their hair for tassels to their garments. In the main, however, each man merely kept count of the number of his human victims, and instead of displaying skulls, wore a red headband whose shade or decoration published his bloody successes. In the southern districts, the persons entitled to these insignia were known as *magani* or *bagani*. The number of victims which a chief of unusual ferocity claimed often ran up to fifty or a hundred. In the mountains of Mindanao as well as among the Moros there still are men living who can boast of such totals. A common man rarely attained to such high distinction. It was the chief who had the backing of followers; who led when the occasion was favorable; and who when peace seemed advisable was in a position to purchase it by the payment of blood money. Theoretically, however, the honor of becoming a *magani* was not restricted to any social class, but depended wholly on a man's individual courage and skill in the use of weapons.

In general, the native attitude is that one violent death calls for another. In the pursuit of this endeavor the balance is often exceeded, and thus instigates fresh reprisals which may go on for generations. This is the principle of what the native calls the "debt of life." It is to him also a debt of honor. Other injuries are readily compoundable, if sufficient payment is tendered; but he who quickly accepts blood money, thereby signifies himself a coward. The consequence is that blood money is as a rule taken only when intent to kill has been lacking, or when a chief's authority is sufficient to enforce a settlement. Where this is the case, blood feuds within the community tend to become rare because of the head man's interests. He not only receives for himself part of the fine that he imposes, but can best maintain his own authority toward neighbors and strangers with an undivided following at his back.

The principle of a fair fight has no meaning to the Filipino. That he possesses a strong sense of justice is evident not only from his well-defined codes of law, but from his general conduct. But once hostilities begin, no quarter is given. The method of slaying is immaterial as long as the end is attained. Most attacks are made from ambush, and as readily upon the aged or women and children as on fighting men. Among the head-hunting tribes no distinction is drawn between skulls of warriors and those of non-combatants, and the attitude of the more southerly *magani* is the same. Often too, once the fighting spirit is roused, little difference is made between the enemy proper and those even remotely associated with him by co-residence in the same region. All the emotional tensity of the East Indian which he so carefully represses in his daily conduct flares up as soon as he draws his *kris*.

The connection between head-hunting and human sacrifice appears to be pretty well established for the Philippines by the fact that the two practices were very nearly mutually exclusive. The northern nationalities preferred head-taking, the central and southern ones sacrifice, but few, if any, followed both customs, and not one, with the exception of the Mohammedans, had reached the point of abandoning both.

Weapons. The prevailing weapons were the spear and the sword, the latter being replaced in parts of the head-hunting area of northern Luzon by the battle ax. In this matter also tribal bent was definite. A group that used the ax employed it consistently and had no swords, and *vice versa*. The ax cannot be said to be the earlier form; but it is that which prevailed among the more primitive tribes possessing least iron and least ability in its manufacture. The various forms of swords have already been described.

The spear in its most ancient form was tipped with bamboo; but wherever iron was sufficiently abundant, the point was replaced by one of that material.

Bows and Blowguns. The bow is often spoken of as if it were the weapon distinctive of the Negrito. It is true that the little black man chiefly relies upon the bow; but he is timid and a hunter rather than a fighter. It by no means follows that because he made much use of it, the brown Filipino did not own the weapon. As a matter of fact, the bow and arrow enjoy very much wider use in the Philippines than it is generally alleged. Artieda in 1576, speaking generally or of the central islands, describes large bows more powerful than those of the English archers; and Chirino and Morga, but little later, refer to the use of bows in some provinces, including certain of the Tagalog districts. The Sambal, until their subjugation, were famous for their skill with the weapon. Among the pagans of Luzon, the Ting-

gian as well as the Ilongot constantly use the bow
and arrow; and the intervening tribes, such as the
Bontok, retain it in the form of a child's toy.   The
Nabaloi and Kankanai were shooting when the
Spaniards first came among them.   At the opposite
end of the archipelago nearly all the uncivilized peoples of Mindanao use arrows for hunting as well as
warfare.   The Mangyan of Mindoro are in the same
class.   Moreover, the word for bow which recurs in
almost every Filipino dialect is a form of the generic
root word common to all the Malayo-Polynesian languages.

It is thus probable that the bow was once as
widely diffused among the brown as among the
black peoples.   The hunting tribes were forced to
cling to its employment, and scarcely learned other
weapons.   Those, on the other hand, that came to
depend upon agriculture, and these in time formed
the majority, had less reason for conservatism, and
among them the spear became established as a
weapon of warfare.   As iron was introduced, the
spear gained in reliability.   Fighting now being at
closer range, the sword or ax became of still greater
value; and in proportion as these tendencies developed and the new weapons improved, the bow was
relegated to special purposes, and in some instances
fell almost wholly into disuse.   In other words, its
history may be inferred to have stood in directly in-
verse relation to that of the iron industry.   The arrow can be but little improved by the use of steel,
and the bow not at all; whereas the lance gains
greatly, and the sword and ax become practicable
weapons only when they are made of metal.

With the comparative importance of iron in all
native life, it might therefore be expected that even

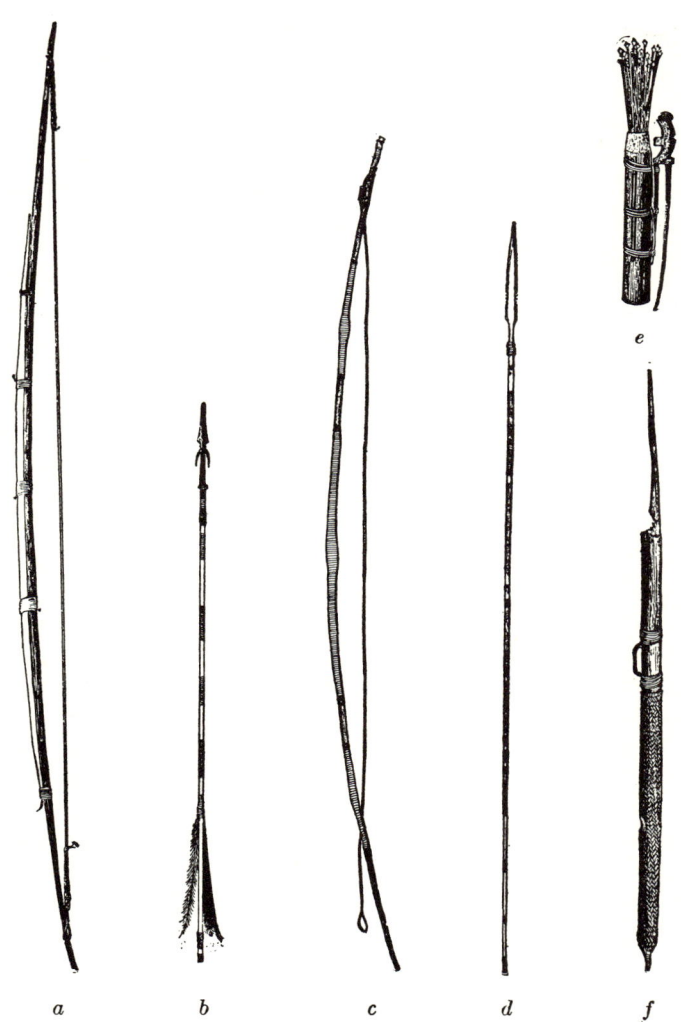

Fig. 31. Propulsive Weapons: *a*, Negrito Bow of Palm Wood; *b*, Negrito Arrow with Iron Point; *c*, Manobo Bow of Bamboo; *d*, Bagobo Arrow with Wooden Head; *e*, Tagbanua Blowgun Darts in Case; *f*, Tirurai Quiver, plaited.

where the bow had been retained it would be a weapon of no very high quality. On the whole this is the fact. It is always a simple self bow, made usually from the wood of the *palma brava* or even of bamboo; is lacking in backing or other reinforcement; and the cord is often of rattan or other vegetable fiber instead of that best of all bowstring materials—sinew. The weapon is long and narrow; among the Negrito it usually exceeds the height of the archer. The arrow is also long, often unfeathered, and rarely provided with other than a hard wooden point. Often the head is detachable, but has a cord affixed and thus really becomes a light harpoon for shooting. The strength of Filipino bows is usually not very great. Even those made by the Negrito fall considerably below their reputation. The arrow releases vary between the Primary, Tertiary, and Mediterranean forms.

The same writers who have dwelled on the bow as the Negrito weapon, have sometimes regarded the blowgun as typically Malayan. This may be partly true, but is certainly not wholly so, since in Palawan the brown-skinned Tagbanua and Negrito Batak both use the weapon. It is known also to the Bagobo and the Yakan Moro; and at the period of discovery seems to have been used more or less generally by the Mindanao tribes, the Bisaya, and perhaps the Tagalog; often with poisoned darts. It is therefore by no means clear to which culture stratum the weapon is to be attributed. It does not seem to be found in northern Luzon.

Shields. The principal defensive weapon is the shield, which is made in three forms that appear to represent as many culture types.

The simplest and presumably earliest of these

Fig. 32. Bisayan Chiefs and Slaves in 1668. From an unpublished
manuscript of Alcina. Courtesy of Philippine Bureau of Science.

types, which is also the most common in Borneo, is a rectangular board sloping somewhat from its middle line toward both the long edges. Seen from the end the shape is therefore that of a low gabled

Fig. 33. Roof-Shaped Northern Type of Rectangular Shield with Exaggerated Prongs. Kalinga.

roof. A boss is either absent or is a mere thickening of the ridge down the middle. At the present time this type of shield is known only from northern Luzon, where its most extreme form is attained among the Tinggian and Kalinga. With these tribes, it is fashioned into three long prongs above and two below. The solid portion is comparatively small, and the weapon is obviously one for parrying rather than receiving missiles. It has even an offensive purpose. In combat, the endeavor is often made to suddenly thrust the three prongs of the upper end against the opponent's legs and with a quick twist trip him up. As soon as he falls, the two prongs at the opposite end are jammed over his neck, pinning his head to the ground and allowing his easy decapitation. Among the Bontok and Nabaloi, the prongs persist, but have become so short and blunt as to leave only shallow scallops between them which can serve no practical purpose, and are obviously decorative. The Ifugao has not even the scallops, but uses a plain rectangular shield. The Apayao shield has a single prong at each end. These project like long spines from the middle ridge of the body of the shield.

The second type prevails in Mindanao, but must once have had a wider distribution, as is shown by the fact that it recurs, at least with its principal features, among the Negritos of Zambales and the Ilongot of Luzon. The general form of this shield is also rectangular. But the long edges are usually scalloped; the ridge is wanting; instead, there is a tendency for the length to be convex; the boss is invariably round. There is considerable inclination to fringe or tassel the edges of the weapon; and some tribes, such as the Bagobo, ornament it with elaborate c a r v i n g s. Many of these features recur in certain shields both of Borneo and Celebes. It is therefore probable that as between this type and the preceding we are dealing with two forms rather widely diffused in the East Indies, and not with mere local developments on Philippine soil. Which of the two

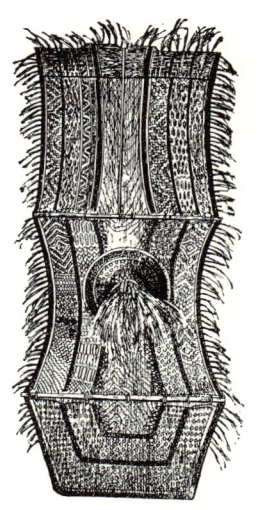

Fig. 34. Southern Type of Rectangular Shield with Scalloped Sides and Fringes. Bagobo.

types is the earlier is not quite certain; but the indication is that the order of development was as here given.

The third type is of entirely different shape, being a round target. This shield is in use among the Moros and is almost certainly of Mohammedan introduction. In fact there can be little doubt that it is a direct Islamic importation from Asia, where the mediaeval Saracen and the Persian and the

Hindu have long used circular bucklers. It is, however, illuminative of the culture history of the Philippines that the Moro, while he adopted the idea of the round shield from more advanced nations, made it over in his own material and therefore in degenerate form. The Asiatic round shield was evolved in leather and metal, but the Filipino, when he took it over, fell back on wood.

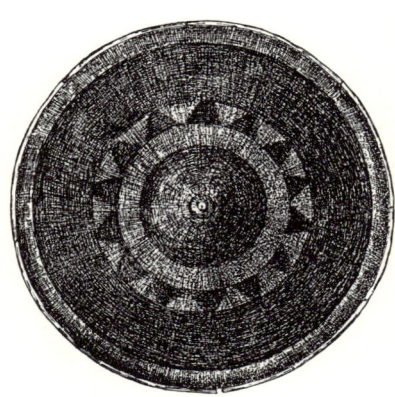

Fig. 35. Circular Type of Shield used by Mohammedans. Samal Moro.

Armor and Firearms. Body armor and helmets were known, but have never been used to any great extent. Rattan helmets such as are worn in Borneo have not been reported from the Philippines. The early Spaniards mentioned body armor made of rattan or cotton quilting—like that worn by the modern Manobo—and corselets of hard black wood. The latter was evidently sleeveless coats of slabs flexibly linked. Similar armor is still sometimes made by the Moros of plates of brass or buffalo horn joined by brass rings. In spite of its weight, it unquestionably affords much protection against swords and spears, but would be useless against firearms.

The Moro also now and then make a brass helmet that appears to be neither of Hindu nor Arabic type, but an imitation of the helmets which were worn by the Spaniards who first invaded the archipelago. It

Fig. 36. Moro Brass Helmet imitated from
an Ancient Spanish Style; and Moro Body Armor
of Buffalo Horn Plates and Brass Links.

183

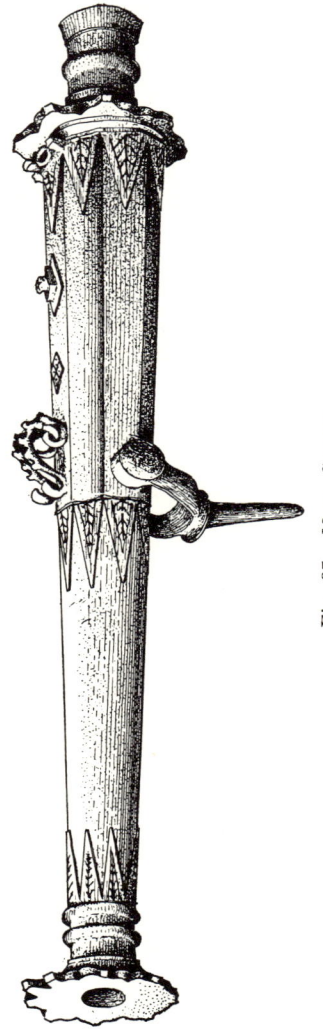

Fig. 37. Moro Cannon.

184

is an interesting example of a local persistence of fashion among a half civilized people.

Firearms had come into the Moro districts of the Philippines along with Mohammedanism. Guns in our sense of the word seem to have been unknown; but every chief of consequence boasted some culverins or small bronze cannons. These were set on the sultans' forts or stockades, and sometimes on war vessels. All these pieces were small, two men usually sufficing for their transport, and mounted on a simple swivel pin. The bore was small, not exceeding an inch or two; and gunpowder both scarce and of poor quality. The Spaniards however praised the quality of workmanship of some of these little cannon, which they believed to have been imported from China. This may have been the case; but the Mohammedans of other parts of the East Indies had used this light artillery for a century or two before, and most of the pieces in use by the Philippine Moros are likely to have been made by Malays. They were not only employed in warfare, but valued as treasures, their esteem among the Moros being similar to that which gongs and Chinese jars enjoyed among the pagans.

Chapter V

RELIGION

Spirits and Gods. The idea that dominates all Filipino religion is the belief in a class of supernatural beings called *anito*. This term is hard to translate, because it includes gods or divinities proper; evil or beneficent spirits of lower rank; and finally the souls of dead human beings. An *anito* is therefore any being which possesses the intelligence of a human person and equal or superior faculties, but lacks a corporeal body. The word is of widespread use in the East Indies and Oceania, and the concept of the *anito* is undoubtedly an extremely ancient one in this part of the world. Its particular meaning varies somewhat from tribe to tribe in the Philippines, some groups thinking rather of gods and spirits, and others primarily of the souls of dead human beings, when they use the term. The Bisaya and peoples of Mindanao generally replace *anito* by the Sanskrit term *diwata* when they refer to a deity or to any supernatural being that has never had a human existence. *Anito* is however the generic term in Tagalog and in a number of other languages, and has become well established in European usage. Some of the Spaniards have gone so far as to describe Filipino religion in general as being a system of *anitería*.

It is significant that the Filipino classes good and evil spirits together as *anito* just as he does not essentially distinguish between the great named gods and the lesser spirits which he recognizes only as classes. It is the fact of supernatural existence without a body that constitutes an *anito,* not particular rank or power or inclination toward moral or immoral acts. It is for the same reason that the souls of the dead are included. No native would dream of thinking of a living man as an *anito;* but once his body is cold and only his soul survives, this soul is not essentially different from those spirits that have never walked the earth in a clothing of flesh. The result is that a sort of ancestor worship prevails. One's father and grandfather have become spirits with the same power of influencing the life of their descendants, as those beings who have always been immaterial. It is even more important in some ways to be on a satisfactory footing with the souls of the dead, since they naturally take a more personal interest in their offspring. A sacrifice is more likely to have weight with them; and on the other hand they are readier to resent neglect.

Some tribes go so far as to believe that the souls of their ancestors have dealings with other spirits, similar to those which men have with one another. They borrow property from them, and when they are unable or unwilling to pay, the creditor spirits, seeing no recourse, attempt to coerce them into settlement by plaguing their living descendants with sickness—exactly as a Filipino who cannot obtain satisfaction from a principal will attempt to take it from his kinsman or dependent. In such case, the living Ifugao must make sacrifices which will extinguish the debt of the dead.

It is clear that the native feels very directly and concretely in these matters, and allows sentimental affection to enter but slightly into his relations with the spirit world. He buys off his ancestors or gods or attempts to ingratiate himself with them; he does not put himself into a frame of mind which we should call truly worshipful. He fears the *anito,* but he is not really humble toward them. The attitude which a devout Christian or Mohammedan or Hindu has toward his god is foreign to him. Nor does he worship his ancestors as a Chinaman worships them with filial piety and respect for their memory. He projects into the spirit world the same conflicting desires and passions and selfishness which exist on this earth, and tries to make his way successful among the *anito* by much the same devices which he uses in his dealings with his fellowmen.

As a point in the history of religious development, it would be very interesting to know whether the Filipino began with an idea of the *anito* as a sort of god and later extended the concept to include lesser spirits and those that were once human; or whether the origin of his faith was a belief in the power of the souls of his dead, and that from this original cult his *anito* concept was extended to include greater spirits and gods. The latter is perhaps the simpler and more plausible hypothesis. But we cannot be sure, since the *anito* religion is undoubtedly ancient even in its present form. Moreover, this type of religious belief is so fundamental in the whole of the East Indies that the problem can only be settled by comparative studies.

The classes of spirits recognized by the Filipino are innumerable and their names often differ from tribe to tribe. There are spirits of the mountains, of the forest, of the water, and so on, *ad infinitum.* Some of these are demons that hunt human beings, or live on corpses, or work mischief in various ways.

Others are protective or at least neutral in their attitude toward humanity, and these when offended can be propitiated, and when they are benevolent can do much to further the affairs of men. Above

these are the great gods, who do not fall into classes like devils or angels, but possess individual personalities and are addressed by their proper names. The number of these is enormously large. The Ifugao, for instance, are said to distinguish several thousand such deities by name.

The greatest gods of all, those who grew first and had a share in shaping the world, are of course fewer; but it is significant that these are less often called upon in actual worship than the minor class divinities. They seem to be thought of as so remote in space or time that their lack of interest in the fortunes of men counterbalances their superior powers. The great gods are frequently grouped into families, or allotted to different layers of the sky, so that they constitute lineages and aeons. Their names show little uniformity, and are generally of native origin.

Fig. 38. Carved Figure of a Spirit. Nabaloi.

But their conception possesses a strong Hindu flavor, and it is probable that although most of these deities were not directly introduced from India, at least the attitude which resulted in their recognition is due to importation. The chief deity of the Tagalog was *Bathala,* which is a native pronunciation of the Sanskrit word for lord, *bhattara.* The Sambal knew their leading divinity as *Akasi,* the Bikol as *Gugurang,* the Bisaya as *Dia Laon,* or *Sidapa.* The origin of these names is not known.

Among the Ilokano and a number of the northern tribes that have remained pagan the chief deity is *Kabunian.* Other divinities or ancient heroes of godlike qualities known to an array of the mountain tribes of Luzon are *Kabigat; Balitok* or "Gold"; *Wigan; Lumawig;* and *Bugan,* the most famous heroine of romance, myth, and prayer.

The Bagobo recognize nine heavens, each with its deity. These are, in order upward, *Lumabat; Salamiawan; Ubnuling; Tiun,* a virgin goddess; *Biat'odan,* wife of *Salamiawan; Bia-ka-pusud-an-langit,* "Lady of the Navel of Heaven"; *Kadeyuna,* younger sister of *Tiun; Malaki Lunsud,* husband of *Kadeyuna;* and *Pangulili,* son of *Ubnuling.* These names are native; the deities are of Hindu type. They are not worshipped, but remain purely literary or mythological concepts. The gods to whom the Bagobo prays and offers are *Pamulak Manobo,* Plant Person, the creator; *Tigyama,* the Protector; *Malaki t'Olu K'Waig,* Hero of the Head of the Waters, who destroys sickness; *Tarabume,* for whom the rice ceremony is held; *Paneyangen,* patron of the brass casters; *Abog,* helper of hunters; *Tagamaling,* who is god and fiend in alternate months; *Mandarangan* of the warriors, to whom human life is offered; and a host of others.

Souls. Holding the settled conviction that human beings become *anito,* it is inevitable that the Filipino must believe in the existence of something spiritual, in other words a soul, in man through his lifetime. He goes farther. He attributes souls to animals; and both in Luzon and Mindanao states expressly that everything in the world has a soul. This idea fits in very nicely with the method of sacrifice. A spirit, being immaterial, would have no use for the substantial portion of whatever was offered to it. It accepts the soul of the sacrifice, leaving the flesh of the victim, or the wine in the jar, for the worshipper's consumption. In the same way, when property is offered, it is merely exposed for a short time on an altar or in a spirit house with the requisite prayer of dedication—then taken back. To leave a valuable object to decay, or deliberately to destroy it, would do the recipient *anito* no good. But the native is logical in these matters and feels that an object that has once been offered and has had its soul put at the disposal of an *anito* is different from other objects. The Bagobo, for instance, who has offered a sword, girds this on again and is free to use it; but he cannot, without great danger of sickness or ill luck from the spirits, sell this sword or allow it to pass into the hands of others.

The Bagobo also attribute two souls to human beings, each inhabiting one side of the body. The left soul frequently leaves the body to roam, and dreams are nothing but its experiences on these wanderings. After death it becomes one of the class of evil spirits known as *buso*, who bring sickness and death to human beings. The right hand soul is the protector and companion of the body, which it never leaves except sometimes to lie on the ground as the shadow falling on the right side of the person. When it separates itself from its fleshly container, death ensues; but the soul is immortal and goes to join its ancestors and companions in the great underground country of the dead.

Sacrifice and Prayer. Sacrifice and prayer are the two forms of ritual in which the Filipino chiefly expresses his religion. The intimate connection between animal sacrifice and the consumption of flesh has already been mentioned: every sacrifice means a feast. So strong is this association that wherever the Filipino has remained pagan he has even reversed the connection, and does not think of slaughtering an animal for food except on the occasion of some ceremony. He feels exactly the same way about his intoxicating liquor of rice or sugar cane. Worship of any consequence being impossible without the offering of this to the gods, drinking and drunkenness have acquired a wholly religious flavor, and are never indulged in on profane occasions or for mere pleasure,—at any rate among the tribes that have kept their ancient faith pure. It is perhaps because of this connection that the Filipino rarely becomes boisterous and never offensively disorderly in his cups. At a ceremony, people urge each other to drink, and take pride in the quantity of liquor which they consume, but restrain themselves within bounds. When the effect of the alcohol becomes overpowering, they go quietly off to sleep. This association of worship with the best things to eat and drink has tended to give Filipino religion a cheerful aspect that largely effaces the dread in which they hold their numerous demons and many of their spirits.

Prayers are of two types: true prayers or direct appeals to the *anito,* and formulas. The formulas are narratives about the gods or ancient heroes. These are recited at the proper occasion, usually

Fig. 39. Religious Sacrifice of a Dog. Bontok.

194

over a sacrifice, in a set form. They recount how a divinity wished to attain some end, or overcome some obstacle, and the means by which he succeeded. It is believed that the recounting of these ancient events, in connection with the sacrifice, helps to bring about a similar outcome among those for whom the recital is made. Very often, therefore, the formula is nothing but a myth with a prayer appended. The Tinggian calls such formulas *diam;* the Ifugao, when they have concluded the narrative proper, go on to a *tulud* or "pushing" in which, by naming place after place, they persuade themselves that they are drawing the gods from their far-away residence to the scene of worship and thereby compel their aid. They usually conclude with some such statement as "not then, but now, not there, but here," to clinch the efficacy of the address.

All this looks like a formidable beginning for an elaborate ritual. In some respects, the Filipino has fulfilled this promise. He often knows from twenty to a hundred different ceremonies; each with its greater or lesser offerings and its appropriate formula or prayers. But on the side of outward and visible expression, his religion has remained undeveloped. Its apparatus is of the simplest, and its symbolism meager. He knows no temples except the little spirit houses that have been described. While he frequently uses altars, these are of the simplest type conceivable: a porcelain bowl set in a split bamboo stick, a coconut shell or plate hung from the rafters, and the like. If an actual offering is made in these, it is a handful of rice, a few betel nuts, or something equally insignificant. Some of the mountaineers of Luzon dispense even with these paraphernalia. The Ifugao seem to use no altars;

the Bontok no spirit house. Their sacrifices are placed on the ground or before the dwelling. Few if any objects are manufactured for express service in worship: an everyday knife or spear or ax dispatches the victim, and the officiator, while he may put on his best, does not don distinctly religious clothing. Symbols of the type of our cross and the Mohammedan crescent, or the cloud terrace of the Pueblo Indians, the Filipino scarcely knows.

Ceremonial Motives. The avowed objects of ritual reflect very neatly the profane ideals of the native. By far the greatest number of ceremonies are held to cure sickness. Often there is a distinct ritual for each recognized disease or type of disease believed to have been caused by one class of spirits.

Allied to these ceremonies are what might be called general welfare rites made by the rich man or chief of the community for the good of all. These are supposed to promote the longevity, general health, and economic prosperity of the group. From these rites it is only a step to the ceremonies previously referred to which are incumbent upon the distinctly rich in order to maintain their prestige and position in society.

Another class of rites are agricultural. As already mentioned, these are almost wholly concerned with rice, other crops evidently being considered as thereby provided for. Very often the agricultural ceremonies were interwoven with other motives. A freshly taken human head promoted the efficacy of the ceremony, which in consequence came to take on the aspect also of a rejoicing over victory. Any ritual able to promote the crops was likely to be considered powerful enough to bring about other desired results as well; and thus often a rite that in origin may have been agricultural is now also a ceremony for health or wealth. There is in fact scarcely a Filipino ritual which does not in some measure subserve more than one purpose.

A thing so important in human careers as marriage required all possible furtherance by religious means from the Filipino point of view. The result was that weddings were even more elaborately ritualized than among ourselves. Often the betrothal and the completion of negotiations or purchase, as well as the final wedding itself, were the occasion of showy and sacred ceremonies. Birth and adolescence went off with very much less attention. But death was again an occasion when religious emotions were awakened. The pagans of Luzon keep the corpse for a considerable period after death, address both it and the spirits repeatedly, and slaughter as large a number of animals as the means of the deceased and his family permit. In Mindanao, the corpse is not kept so long, but a funerary ceremony is also held on a great scale, either soon after death or at the conclusion of mourning.

Religious Officials. There are no official priests for the conduct of religion among the modern pagans. There are persons recognized as possessing religious power; but they hold this in virtue of personal ability, not as members of a caste or profession. Essentially, therefore, they are medicinemen or mediums rather than true priests, although the recitation of prayers and formulas is largely left to them. Any person endowed with the power of trance or ventriloquistic communication with the spirits sufficient to impress his listeners, is accepted as one of these mediums. Old and young, men and women, share indifferently in the office; in fact among the majority of the tribes women seem to have been more successful in this capacity. The medium frequently holds seances with the spirits, calling them by name, asking them questions and causing them to answer. Such sessions take place in the darkened house. With the Ifugao the medium becomes possessed by a god during the public and open air conduct of a ceremony and speaks as the god. Often the mediums learn from older ones, or there is a kind of initiation; but the chief condition of their recognition seems to be inborn power. They have been most frequently described under their Tagalog name of *katalonan* or by the Bisayan designation *bailan*. Other tribes use different terms, but the institution remains substantially the same. It is undoubtedly a very ancient element of Filipino and general East Indian religion.

The ritual features here outlined apply most directly to the pagans of Mindanao and Luzon and the Tagalog and Bisaya, although among the latter the old cults, except for a few survivals, have long since died out before Christianity. The Moro too has effaced most of his old worship under the sway of Mohammedanism. The religion of the Negritos and of the primitive groups on outlying islands, such as the Mangyan and Tagbanua, is unfortunately very little known. Its forms are probably less elaborate than those of the Luzon and Bisayan nationalities, but all the bits of available evidence point to its being of the same type.

Magic and Medicine. Like all nations who have not some measure of science in their thinking, the Filipinos are given to magical practices and beliefs. Also as usual, the dividing line between magic and religion is impossible to draw. Every sacrifice involves, in a sense, magical power, and the formulas that push or compel the gods to do the will of the worshipper fall in the same category. Conversely, a charm or fetish is never thought to be efficacious merely through its own directly inherent virtues. It always stands in some connection, immediate or remote, with the god, spirit, or soul.

Medicine is a case in point. The Bagobo attribute the majority of severe illnesses to the operations of evil spirits called *buso,* who live on the flesh of corpses and therefore are constantly employing every means in their power to procure food for themselves by causing the death of human beings. Often, the *buso* enters the body of his intended victim. There he remains, unless expelled, until death ensues, when he flies away rejoicing in anticipation of the feast that awaits him on the victim's interment. In other cases he is believed not to need to enter the patient's body, but to be able to work him harm from a distance. Other diseases the Bagobo declare to be brought on by a breach of taboo, that is the violation of some magic rule. Among such trespasses are the disposal of an object once devoted to the gods by sacrifice; the selling of even the most ordinary piece of cloth before it is entirely completed; the wearing by a young man of the type of jacket reserved for the old, or of the head piece dyed in the color for successful warriors; planting rice in any other direction than southward; laughing at one's own reflection in the water; or winding a brass girdle about one's waist an odd instead of an even number of times. When none of these explanations seem appropriate, the Bagobo attributes his suffering to the experiences of his soul, or rather to the left-hand one of his two souls. He says that the soul jumps into a river and his body aches in the abdomen; the soul strikes his head against a tree, pain in the corporeal head is the result; a sore mouth may be the result of the soul drinking boiling water.

The methods of curing disease are as various as the beliefs concerning its origin. The gods are prayed to and given sacrifices. The afflicting *buso* spirit himself may sometimes be bought off in Bagobo belief by an offering of betel nut. Little figures are slung on the necklace of a child with the idea of drawing the *buso* spirit out of the body into the manikin. Again, a priest-medium is sometimes summoned who has recourse to a ceremonial sprinkling of water on the joints of the patient, or prescribes cinnamon bark, crow liver, snake bile, or some similar medicine. Very frequently the remedial substance is burned to ashes which are drunk with a quantity of hot water. At other times the hot ashes are merely laid upon the diseased part. This shows quite clearly that the native attitude regarding such medicinal substances is that they operate magically rather than pharmaceutically. That this is the basis of belief is also clear from another treatment sometimes given patients: they are made to inhale the smoke from a burning nest of the *limokun* bird. The efficacy of this treatment rests on the fact that the bird is endowed with magical power—he is the omen bird above all others. The smoke is only the means of conveying his beneficial supernatural qualities to the sick person.

No two tribes follow exactly the same practices; what is taboo to one is often freely permitted among the other. One may recognize certain causes of disease and cures for them of which the other is totally unaware. But however much the specific beliefs and acts vary, the general basis is everywhere identical, and the foregoing sketch of Bagobo magic and medicine may therefore be taken as substantially representative of the psychology of all the Philippine peoples.

Taboos. Taboos against personal activity are observed by every people in the archipelago. Almost always they are laid on mourners for the dead, but often are imposed also when disease breaks out or other unfavorable or critical junctures arise. Usually the taboo operates by forbidding, so far as possible, both work and enjoyment, and the consumption of wine, rice, and other choice foods. Such a taboo rarely expires automatically. When it has run its proper period, it is formally lifted by a ceremony of some sort. If the occasion is sufficiently important, such a rite of termination almost always involves a sacrifice—perhaps even that of human life, either in combat or as a formal offering. Even the most primitive of the Filipinos, however, are much less inclined to apply such taboos on the occasion of birth and particularly adolescence than many other primitive peoples. In spite of its considerable prevalence, also, the taboo idea is probably not so developed or powerful in the Philippines, nor anywhere in the East Indies for that matter, as in the Polynesian and Melanesian islands of the Pacific.

Omens and Divination. On the other hand omens play a disproportionately large part in Filipino life. Natural omens are exceedingly numerous. An animal of a particular species runs across the path and a journey is postponed. A ceremony must be promptly abandoned if an earthquake occurs, else the giver of the rite will surely die. A rotten tree crashing to the ground at night is a portent of death. Dozens if not hundreds of such omens could be cited. Sometimes a charm or prayer is believed sufficient to avert the indicated event; but in many cases there is no recourse, according to the native point of view, but to delay or wholly renounce whatever undertaking is on foot.

For every important enterprise, such as attacks by war parties, marriages, and the like, omens were deliberately sought by means of special ceremonies. Every tribe that has to any considerable extent preserved its ancient religion appears to have one or more such divinatory rites. A stone or piece of iron or firebrand may be suspended and the direction or manner of its swinging read as prophetic of the future; or a stick is stood up and allowed to fall; or the priest-medium may study the reflections or images in a vessel of water. Often the method is that of question and answer. Names are recited, or direct queries put, until a sign is thought to be given by the omen object. When a Nabaloi falls ill, the priest-medium mentions the various classes of spirits that might have produced the disease until the response is obtained. The cause of the sickness having been in this way determined, the cure is effected by making the offering and ceremony that are appropriate to the particular spirits. Similar procedures are followed when it is desired to find lost objects or to discover a thief.

Some form of ordeal serving the detection of theft, or even the determination of guilt between two persons mutually accusing each other, was observed by most Philippine peoples; and a variety of devices serving this purpose were worked out among the various tribes—all of them believed to be infallible. Some of these have already been mentioned in the section on native law.

Another type of prediction is palm reading, known to the Tirurai as *fengintuanan,* and practised also by the Bagobo with attention to lines of life, wealth, and the like, rather similar to the indications recognized in our own system. That palmistry has been reported only from Mindanao suggests that it is a relatively recent importation, possibly an accompaniment of Islam.

Perhaps the most interesting of all the many forms of divination prevailing in the Philippines are two types familiar to us from the religion of the ancient Greeks and Romans: augury or the foretelling of the future by the flight and actions of birds, and haruspicy or prediction by the examination of the internal organs of slaughtered animals. In the southern Philippines a species of pigeon known as the *limokun* is the favorite omen bird. In northern Luzon, smaller species known as *tuttut, pitpit, ichu,* and so on, are favored. The liver and bile sack of the pig are the internal organs most frequently inspected. The color, shape, or size of these are portentous in much the same way as the appearance of the omen bird on the right or left side of the observer, its behavior, or its call.

Unfortunately, the details of these methods of divination have been less fully recorded in the Philippines than in Borneo; or else Filipino practices were in themselves less elaborate. Nevertheless, all the evidence available suggests that the existence of these types of foretelling in the East Indies is no mere interesting coincidence, but that the practices are directly and historically connected with those of the ancient Mediterranean peoples. Hepatoscopy, the particular method of divination by means of the liver of sacrificial animals, has been shown to have originated in Babylonia; at least, its earliest recorded occurrence was there. From there the custom spread with little modification to surrounding parts of the world. Westward, it was carried to the Etruscans, and from this people the Romans derived it at an early date. For the transmission to the East Indies, there is a gap in our knowledge; but the general type of procedure is identical. For augury the case is less complete; but the association between this form of foretelling and liver divination both in pagan Roman and in the East Indies, suggests rather powerfully that the two allied sets of practices have traveled over large parts of the world in company. There seems something rather non-Hindu about both of them; and yet it is conceivable that these methods of divination may at some time have attached themselves to Hindu religion and have been transmitted along with it. It is not unlikely that they entered the East Indies and the Philippines in companionship with animal sacrifice.

In any event, a vast perspective is opened up. The modern Filipino mountaineer and the Roman of twenty-five hundred years ago practised the same customs not because their minds worked identically and automatically produced the same reaction, but because both were subjected to common historical influences—both of them subjected, although at far-removed times and places, to the same currents of civilization. With two or three instances of such common origin established, it is probable that there must have been a strong tendency for many other elements of culture to be transmitted, and little doubt that time and again the tendency became realized.

From this broader point of view, then, Filipino civilization, in fact all East Indian civilization, is far from being an entity in itself. It constitutes only one phase of the infinitely more ancient and complex civilization that has for ages prevailed from Europe to the middle of the Pacific Ocean, and which can be fully understood only as an interrelated composite. The underlying problem of Philippine culture is not what is distinctly native about it or how it came to be so, but what is Chinese and Indian, Polynesian and Arab, and Greek and Roman in it; just as the cultures of all these groups cannot be fully comprehended as detached units, but if insight is desired must be looked upon as mere fragments of a vast whole that far transcends any one of them.

Mythology. Filipino myths and tales are a strange composite of Indian and primitive Malaysian constituents. The Javanese and peninsular Malay have taken over Hindu epics and romances. The Filipino has not; but the ultimate Indian origin of much of the content of his traditions is undeniable. The permeating influence of the greater civilization long ago reached him, but not with its full brunt. It evidently filtered through in bits and at second or third hand. Before the more luxuriant products of Hindu imagination, native invention gave way at point after point. Yet the continuity of native life as a whole being undisturbed by any great shock, the lower civilization of the islands remained the recipient organism, as it were, which re-received and assimilated and worked over the more exalted literary plots and religious concepts that came into it piecemeal.

Heroic Romances. The Philippine nationality whose mythology is best known is the Tinggian, a people never wholly out of contact with the coast and yet maintaining their ancient paganism to the present. The longest and finest of their tales can only be described as romances of battle, love, magic, hidden births, intrigue, and other adventure cast in the heroic mould. The actors are *Aponi-tolau,* the great warrior, and *Aponi-bolinayen,* whom he marries; his sister *Aponi-gawani* and *Aponi-bolinayen's* brother, *Aponi-balagan,* between whom a second love story is spun; their parents and sons; and innumerable monsters, mythical beings, and enemies. The chief personages appear under a great variety of names, but are always identified as the same. Each narrator recounts his tale differently, so that the stories frequently overlap in incidents, and yet possess a total variety sufficient to have made possible their combination into a great coherent cycle. This unification into one great epic the Tinggian, however, never accomplished. This failure would be enough, even if other indications were lacking, to suggest that he had never come into direct contact with the Hindu; since the latter at an ancient time developed the faculty of combining vast numbers of episodes into a long plot. On the other hand, the primary motives of these Tinggian romances are love and fighting, and suggest very strongly that these tales are not the uninfluenced product of a naïvely primitive culture; since really uncivilized people, whether they fight or love much or little, almost invariably concern themselves but slightly with these subjects in their traditions.

A further indication of the blended quality of the Tinggian romances is afforded by the nature of the personages. These are distinctly human—glorified human beings indeed—but clearly neither gods placed high and serene above the affairs of men, nor on the other hand the indeterminately animal or half animal characters that characteristically populate the mythology of wholly uncivilized peoples.

There is a perceptible although simple literary style in these stories. The plot moves swiftly and yet with frequent touches of the fuller treatment which cultivated literary narration demands. Stock expressions abound as freely as stock sentiments and incidents. Characterization, in the modern sense, remains extremely rudimentary, but some success is evinced in portraying or suggesting emotions.

Formulas. The second type of narratives are called *diam* by the Tinggian and are formulas recited as part of ceremonies. Possessing therefore a distinctly practical purpose, they are much less imaginative than the romances as well as briefer; and as a rule they confine themselves pretty strictly to the business in hand. Thus the formula recited in the *sayang* tells how the people formerly celebrated this rite erroneously, until instructed by the deity *Kadaklan* to watch a correct performance. After this the spirits came in greater numbers and the rite resulted more efficaciously.

The Nabaloi and Ifugao possess a less developed cycle of romances, but embroider their ritualistic formulas with many of the episodes of adventure and interest in the hero's fortunes and personality which the Tinggian reserve for their romances.

Explanatory Myths. A third type of traditions comprises myths proper, that is, stories of origin, explanation, and supernatural experience. In these

are recounted the origin of the earth, of the sun and
moon, of fire, the history of the flood, the cause of
death, the reasons for the shapes and habits of animals and birds, the origin of peculiar stones, and
similar matters. Many of these tales are explanatory nature myths such as are typical of primitive
peoples. They draw little line between the spiritual
and the human, the human and the animal, the ani-
mate and the inanimate. They do not to any great
extent personify the elements and forces of nature
in the manner of the mythology of the Greeks,
Egyptians, Babylonians, or Hindus. In fact, like
nearly all origin myths of truly primitive nations,
they have little connection with ritual, and practically none with the worship of personalized deities.
The Tinggian tales of this type are brief and rather
bald and usually consist of a single episode not
brought into relation with any others of the same
type. For instance, a flood comes and Fire takes
refuge in bamboo, stones, and iron. This is the reason it can still be extracted from these substances.
Again, the spirit *Kaboniyan* enters the body of a
woman to teach her how to cure illness and how to
farm. From her the people derive their knowledge
of these arts. At a significant moment a dog kills a
cock and *Kaboniyan* informs her that this means
that death has entered the world. Another tale accounts for the monkey, who was once a man given to
leaning on his planting stick instead of working
continuously.   The stick grew into a tail and he
went off as the animal. Other narratives relate the
experience of human beings with spirits and demons, usually with an implied moral from which
the hearers can profit. Thus it is told how people
failed to lay iron and a certain vine on the grave of

a dead person; whereupon a spirit immediately observed the omission and stole away the body. It is
clear that these myths constitute a kind of elemen-
tary substitute for the two things that we call science and moralizing. They not only attempt to sat-
isfy curiosity as to the causes that shape the world,
but point out the lines of conduct that are respectively profitable and inexpedient.

The rather fragmentary nature of these explanatory myths is typical of other Philippine tribes; but
occasionally some idea is singled out for more elaborate treatment. Thus the majority of the Luzon
mountaineers tell at length of a great ancient flood
from which only a brother and sister escaped.
They married and after a series of adventures re-
populated the world. This tale has been recorded
so frequently and with so many variations that it
has clearly obtained a primary hold on the mythological imagination of an entire series of tribes, and
appears to be one of the most fundamental traditions known to the Filipinos. It was told, for instance, by the ancient Bisaya, of whose mythology
and that of the Tagalog only some slight fragments
have been preserved. It is known, however, that
these great nations brought their accounts of origins
into connection with genealogies of gods, heroes,
and probably personal ancestors.

Fables. A fourth class of tales are fables, usually
with animal actors, and similar in many ways to
those familiar in our own civilization, except for
the fact that they avoid the specific pointing of a
moral. Trickery is one of the motives most emphasized. Thus the Tinggian relate how turtle and
monkey planted bananas, the former in the ground
but the ape by hanging them up. Of course, turtle

alone grew a crop; but, being unable to climb his tree, sent monkey up to secure the fruit. Instead, monkey devoured it and then went comfortably to sleep. Turtle revenged himself by frightening monkey and causing him to fall to his death on sharp points which he had set around the tree; and then sold his flesh to other monkeys. When however he subsequently taunted them as cannibals, they caught and prepared to execute him. He convinced them, by pointing to the marks on his shell, that cutting and burning could not hurt him; whereupon they tried to drown him. When he emerged from the water with a fish, they became enthusiastic at the unforeseen prospect and attempted to imitate him, but lost their own lives.

Another tale relates the race of buffalo and shell. After buffalo has run a distance he calls to his competitor, whose place is taken by another shell that answers for him. The buffalo, thinking that he has not yet outdistanced his rival, runs again and again until he falls dead from exhaustion.

Little stories of this type are told in very similar form among every people in the islands and many have been found in Borneo and elsewhere in the East Indies. Some are quite demonstrably of Hindu origin, and all are cast in a Hindu mould. Inasmuch as many of our own fables are also known to be of Indian origin or patterned on Hindu examples, or have been taken by the Hindus from our ancestors, it is not surprising that these tales from the Philippines have a strangely familiar ring in our ears. It is no wonder, since both we and the Filipinos have derived them from common sources.

Chapter VI

KNOWLEDGE AND ART

Astronomy. From what has been said of his mythology, it is clear that the uncivilized Filipino could not have possessed much of what we are wont to name scientific knowledge. Yet some rudiments of astronomy and other branches of knowledge existed among the most backward groups. The pagans of southern Mindanao distinguish several constellations, and determine the season for beginning rice planting by the appearance of *poyo-poyo,* probably the Pleiades, and *balatik,* Orion. From Luzon several calendars have been reported; that is, names of recognized divisions of the year. There is some doubt whether each new moon receives an appellation of its own, or whether the terms refer to less definite periods. They designate seasons or seasonal occupations, especially with reference to agriculture. Even if these calendars are really lunar, they must be of quite a primitive type, because twelve lunations do not coincide with the year and they contain no indication of any regulated method of correction.

As regards the sun, moon, and planets, the Filipinos hold only the fanciful concepts of mythology, except where the superior wisdom of the Hindus has reached them. They share, for instance, in the world-wide primitive belief that eclipses are caused by a monster that attempts to devour the moon, and can be frightened off by shouts and noises. But the particular form which this belief takes among them is distinctly Indian: the monster is a giant bird that bears the Hindu name *rahu*. An even more specific importation is the observance by the Magindanao Moro of five divisions of the day designated Mahesvara, Kala, Sri, Berma, Bisnu—the slightly altered names of famous Hindu deities. These periods, which appear to be based on the visible planets, are used in written astrological divination. It is of special interest to find this precise relic of Hindu astronomy maintained among a Mohammedan people. It is likely that the introduction of Arabic writing was the cause of the preservation of the Indian practice.

Use of Numbers. As regards the mathematical abilities of the Filipino we are unfortunately little informed. It is practically certain that he had no idea of geometry or any of the other abstract branches of the science, and contented himself with simple arithmetical operations. He did, however, add and subtract numbers considerably larger than those which most uncivilized people are accustomed to deal with; and while it is doubtful whether he possessed any system of multiplication as such, he followed it in effect in his schemes of values, in which five, twenty-five, fifty, five hundred, and a thousand units received special designations. This is the Bontok plan: the Tagalog and Bisaya may have had a more refined one. Such a system does not make for mathematical insight in our sense, but is capable of astounding utility for arithmetical operations; very much as among ourselves a person inadequately equipped in formal arithmetic sometimes operates easily and correctly with large sums of money through knowing the relative values of coins. With his keen property sense, and his possessions rated accurately as well as highly, the Filipino had of course to possess such a practical faculty.

The purely native stratum of religion appears to be free from marked preference for any symbolic or ritualistic number. The Bagobo consider even numbers lucky and odd ones unlucky; except nine, which is always good. This is a point of view characteristic of European and Asiatic civilization, and therefore presumably imported. Really primitive people rarely have any feeling for odd or even, but fix on a certain number, such as four or seven, as being the most complete and perfect one, and then bring it into their ceremonials and beliefs at every possible opportunity. This is not a Filipino habit.

Sanskrit Loan Words. It would be very strange if the many pieces of knowledge that were carried from India into the Philippines had entered without bringing in their names at least sometimes. This has actually happened; and all the lowland Filipino dialects contain a stock of Sanskrit words. Several of these have already been mentioned in connection with one or another phase of religion. From the coast a fraction of these words have spread to the interior districts, at any rate in the south. In northern Luzon words of Sanskrit origin are rare and perhaps wholly lacking, except as they may have been imported in recent centuries by the intrusive Ilokano. The mountain region of this island has been in every way the part of the Philippines least subject to Hindu influence.

As regards the greater nationalities, it is rather remarkable that the number of Sanskrit words is about twice as great in Tagalog as in Bisaya and the Mindanao dialects, in spite of the greater proximity of the latter to Borneo. This difference can scarcely be wholly explained away as due to our more perfect knowledge of Tagalog. It seems likely that the latter people received their loan words, and with them a considerable body of Indian culture, through direct contact with the Malay Peninsula or the coast of Indo-China which they front across the China Sea; and that another Sanskrit element penetrated Mindanao and the Bisayan islands by way of Borneo. Subsequently the two sections are likely to have transmitted to each other part of the cultural and linguistic elements which each had received separately. Since words persist so tenaciously, if at all, that their original sources can usually be determined with certainty, whereas customs and ideas are constantly made over until their origin becomes much more doubtful, the prosecution of accurate philological study in the Philippines promises to throw much light on the exact history of Indian and East Indian contacts with the archipelago.

How far linguistic analysis may go in unravelling history can be illustrated from a quotation from Pardo de Tavera. The words which Tagalog borrowed from Sanskrit he says, "are those which signify intellectual acts, moral conceptions, emotions, superstitions, names of deities, of planets, of numerals of high number, of botany, of war and its results and conclusions, and finally of titles and dignities, some animals, instruments of industry, and the names of money." From this he goes on to argue that Hindus must have been present in the Philippines in person, and at least among the Tagalog filled the principal positions of power and prestige: "the warfare, religion, literature, industry, and agriculture were at one time in the hands of the Hindus." This is perhaps an exaggerated inference. East Indians saturated with Hindu civilization could just as well have produced the same effects in the Philippines. But it is clear that the effects occurred; and it will be only a matter of more patient and critical study to trace them with considerable accuracy, and perhaps even determine their period quite closely.

Writing. With the Sanskrit words came a form of writing based on the Sanskrit alphabet. This was not only considerably modified, but much abbreviated, yet the connection is perfectly clear. The Tagalog wrote with three signs for vowels and twelve for consonants; which, with the simple phonetic character of his tongue, sufficed. In reality, this script was a syllabary rather than an alphabet. The vowels were written only when they stood alone or at the beginning of words. Each consonant sign stood for the consonant followed by the sound *a*. A mark or point above changed the vowel of the syllable to *e* or *i*, and the same point below the character caused it to be sounded with the vowel *o* or *u*. The Bisaya, Pampanga, and other nations followed a similar system of writing, and only the Mohammedans came to use Arabic script, which is much less adapted to the genius of the Malayan languages. The alphabets of Hindu origin have long since gone out of use among all the Christian nations, who now employ the ordinary Roman letters with their Spanish values. Two distinctly primitive people, however, the Mangyan of Mindoro and some of the Tagbanua of Palawan, have preserved forms of this ancient writing. The Mangyan write horizontally from left to right; the Tagbanua in vertical columns reading from top to bottom and the columns following in order from right to left. The latter seems to have been the method also of the Tagalog. The inscriptions consist of incisions in the surface of strips of bamboo. The Tagbanua alphabet betrays its close affiliation to the Tagalog letters as they have been preserved in the handwriting of Father Chirino; although in the accompanying figure (40) the latter have been turned one-quarter way round from their proper position in the column.

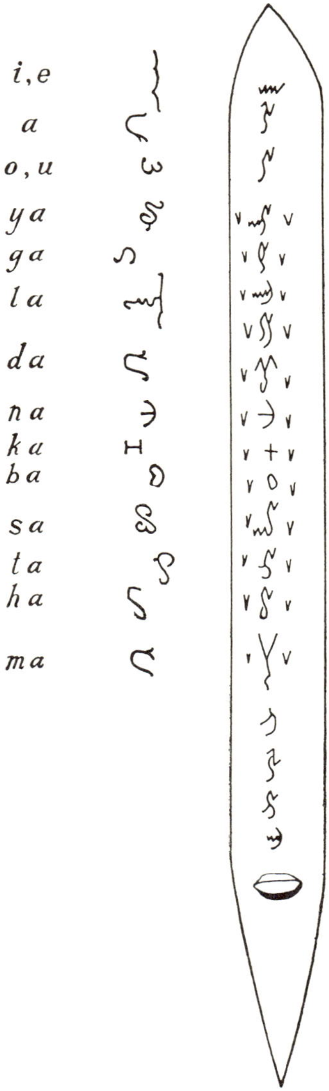

With the Mangyan and Tagbanua still maintaining their ancient system of writing, it seems almost certain that the mountaineers of Luzon— some of whom have been

Fig. 40. Philippine Syllabaries. To right, modern Tagbanua characters incised on a slip of bamboo. Middle, ancient Tagalog characters, turned to show similarity to the Tagbanua ones (the Tagalog characters come into proper position if the column is read as a horizontal line). Left, value of the characters in Roman letters.

even less exposed to Spanish contacts—would have done the same if they had ever possessed such a system. The inference that they have always been illiterate coincides with other indications that stamp them as being that group of Filipinos (other than the Negrito) who have preserved the primitive pre-Hinduized Malaysian culture in its greatest purity.

Art. On the side of plastic and depictive art, the Filipino cannot be accorded the right to high rank. He does pleasingly decorate useful objects such as cloth, mats, and metal work, but he rarely goes beyond mere surface ornamentation, and if he does his efforts are almost invariably crude. His most pretentious artistic achievements, such as steel and brass chasing and the textile patterns produced by dyeing in parts, have already been described, and are obviously due to foreign influence. The contrast between his own scantily and simply decorated pottery and the finely glazed wares which he received from China is very striking. The cloth which he weaves according to his own devices usually bears only the simplest patterns, such as stripes. His house has remained utilitarian, with scarcely even a rudimentary endeavor at ornament. The *anito* figures or idols which he once used in religion and which the mountaineer of Luzon still sometimes carves, were rude: a suggestion of the human figure in abbreviated conventionalized form without aesthetic aspiration sufficed all needs. Pictures as such the Filipino seems never to have attempted. Altogether he stands well below the Polynesian in the development of his art; and this is the more remarkable because industrially he was at least equal and economically much more advanced.

Fig. 41. Patterns incised on Bamboo Lime Boxes. Bagobo.

218

Music. Native music had reached the point of possessing a number of instruments of the three types generally recognized: percussion, wind, and string. The Mohammedan tribes, and those who have come under their influence, possess not only xylophones, but sets of gongs on which melodies can be played or accompanied. These instruments are almost certainly not of home invention. Throughout almost all the islands a sort of guitar is found. This is made of a joint of bamboo from which several cords of the surface fiber have been slit loose

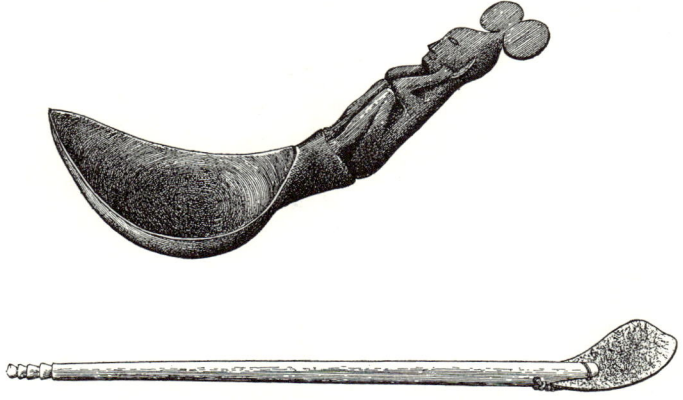

Fig. 42. Ifugao and Negrito (lower) Spoons, illustrating the upper and lower degrees of plastic decoration achieved by the Filipino in carving.

except at the ends. These cords are then given tension by being elevated on bridges. Even the Negritos use this instrument. More elaborate stringed instruments of obviously Asiatic form have penetrated to such pagan tribes as the Bagobo. A sort of jew's harp or tuning fork cut in a sliver of bam-

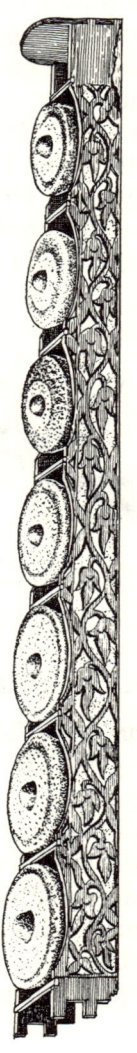

Fig. 43. Moro Musical Instrument consisting of a Set of Graduated Gongs on a Carved Wooden Frame.

220

boo has almost universal distribution and is particularly used in courtship. It does not carry enough
volume for public performance. Simple flutes are
also widely diffused. They are straight tubes without a reed, blown from the end: the Negrito sometimes holds them to the nose.

These instruments as collected in museums theoretically afford a means of determination of the
scale or scales that underlie Filipino music, but unfortunately the practical obstacles to such procedure
are great. The strings very quickly get out of tune,
and in a set of gongs it is quite possible that mechanical insufficiency leads the native musician
sometimes to accept several pieces which he feels
to be somewhat improperly pitched. It is therefore
necessary to depend upon notations of native music,
and of these very few have as yet been made. The
Nabaloi do seem to follow a fairly definite scale,
substantially the same as our melodic minor, but
with the fundamental tone in the middle and its ordinary range to the fifth above and below, or but
little more than an octave over all. The Moro gong
sets have a range of one and a half to two octaves,
but the few that have been examined differ, so that
the musical scheme on which they are put together
remains uncertain. The rhythms of the vocal music seem everywhere to be rather simple, and the
structure of songs equally so. Considerably more
elaborate melodies are known from distinctly primitive people in several other parts of the world. On
the whole, the Filipino is not given to much singing
except on the occasion of gatherings and celebra-
tions, and then his song is almost always accompanied by instrument and dance. The constant use

Fig. 44. Warriors and Houses, probably Bisayan, 1668. From an unpublished manuscript of Alcina. Courtesy of Philippine Bureau of Science.

of tuned or tunable instruments by many tribes cannot but have had some effect on their singing, so that the ancient type of essentially vocal music is likely to have been preserved in aboriginal purity only among the Negritos and some of the brown-skinned pagans of Luzon.

CHAPTER VII

SUMMARY AND CONCLUSIONS

IF now we attempt to draw to a head the many
threads that have been followed through the preceding pages, we find conclusions something like
this:—

The three aspects under which groups of human
beings can be considered—their physique or race,
their speech, and their life or civilization—do not
yield coincident pictures for the Philippines. They
must therefore be reviewed separately, as in so
many other parts of the world.

Racially, three varieties of man occur in the
islands, besides the intrusive Europeans and Chinese of recent centuries. One of these three varieties, the Negrito, is of Negroid affinities and a
dwarf race. The two others, the Indonesian and
the Malaysian, are both Mongoloid—the former less,
the latter more specifically so; the difference between them is not very great, although indubitable.
These three races or sub-races reached the Philippines in the order named. The region of the source
of the Negritos is wholly unknown. The origin of
the Indonesians and Malaysians appears to have
been in southern Asia, although the time and route
of their arrivals remain questionable.

On the side of language, the peoples of the Philippines do not break up into well marked groups, but
without exceptions speak forms of a single mother
tongue, the Malayo-Polynesian that prevails over
most of the East Indies and Oceania. The local varieties of this within the Philippines are not so dif-

225

ferent but that they may well have developed on the spot.

Civilization is more complex than either population or speech, comprising at least half a dozen strains or streams of different source.

The earliest of these culture forms is that carried by the Negrito on his arrival in the islands. This must have been excessively simple and has not been able to maintain itself through several thousand years of contact and competition with more advanced types of civilization. The customs of the Negrito of today are an abridged copy of the customs of the other islanders. Only the Negrito attitude toward life, his habits as contrasted with his customs, his social psychology as distinct from the content of his social activity, seem to be a remnant of his aboriginal mode of life.

Primitive Indonesian culture has also not been preserved intact. Its best surviving representation is found among the pagan mountain inhabitants of northern Luzon; but even this culture has assimilated much from those that followed it. Indonesian civilization appears to have maintained itself with less change in the domain of social and familiar fabric than on the side of industry, invention, knowledge, and belief.

The culture of the Malaysians who followed the Indonesians may at first have been very similar to that of the latter but has subsequently become heavily tinctured by absorption of elements of Indian civilization; or it may have been pretty well Hinduized before its earliest carriers reached the Philippines. A finer analysis than is at present possible will be needed to resolve this alternative.

The Indonesian culture and at least part of the

Malaysian culture are characterized by one feature which needs to be fully recognized before their place in the world's history is intelligibly estimable: the non-Hindu basis thereof is not merely East Indian; it is also Indo-Chinese. To put the case differently, Indo-China and the East Indies at one time, subsequent to the supposed prevalence of the Negritos and prior to the first arrival of specific Hindu influences, seem to have harbored an essentially common culture which varied locally of course, but, so far as can now be judged, not very significantly. This culture, both on the mainland of Asia and in the archipelago, was overlaid in many areas by civilizational imports from higher centers. Some of these imports were the results of invasions, as by the Burmese and Tai peoples in Indo-China and by Sumatrans, Malays, and Arabs in the East Indies. Wherever in Indo-China and Malaysia much of the early culture has been preserved, we find peoples whose customs show affinity to those of the Luzon highlanders. Where the early culture has been more mixed with subsequent imports, there are resemblances to the culture for instance of the pre-Spanish Tagalog and Bisaya. In other words, Indo-China and all the East Indies seem once to have constituted a single culture area, and wherever they have remained relatively primitive, still constitute one.

The following list of cultural traits common repectively to several peoples of the Philippines, of the remainder of the East Indies, and of Assam or other parts of the Indo-Chinese mainland, makes concrete the underlying uniformity: *kaingin* agriculture; rice terraces; meat consumption chiefly in connection with sacrifice; betel chewing; gabled thatch houses raised from the ground; tree houses; bark cloth; cotton; tie-dyeing of warps; brimless caps; wearing of combs; tooth-filing; tattooing; fire cord or saw; fire piston; vertical piston bellows; gongs of bronze or brass considered valuables; bow of bamboo; blowgun; girls' house; religious festivals given to promote or preserve one's social status; head hunting; human sacrifice; bamboo altars; cult of ancestral spirits; divination; plurality of souls.

In the last analysis, therefore, the primitive or native culture of the Philippines can be understood only as a fragmentarily surviving part of an ancient "Southeast Asiatic" culture in which mainland and islands shared alike.

The Indian influences are on the whole perhaps the most profound that have affected Philippine civilization. Two circumstances are of importance regarding them. First, there seem to have been carried with them a number of culture elements whose ultimate origin was not Hindu but Western: the use of iron, religious divination, and sacrifice, for instance. Secondly, at least the bulk and perhaps all of the Indian importation took place through the mechanism not of Hindus but of more or less Hinduized Malaysians who visited or settled the Philippines from other parts of the East Indies.

Chinese civilization affected the Philippines later and much more sparingly than Indian. The significant trait of Chinese relations is that they introduced materials and products, but few if any ideas or institutions.

Mohammedanism cut deep, but began to come late —little more than five centuries ago,—spread over only a small part of the islands, and was then almost completely arrested by the Spaniards. Law, knowledge, writing, political organization, some handicrafts, were thoroughly made over in the south of the archipelago in the wake of this dominating religious cult.

The Spaniards gave a semi-European impress to the life of nine-tenths of the Philippine people. They introduced Catholicism and letters and caused considerable remodelling of economic and industrial conditions, besides enabling a steady and large increase of population.

The changes due to Americans have been great, considering the few years involved. These changes may be summarized as having been specially effective in the direction of bringing the more backward nationalities of the islands nearer participation in contemporaneous Western civilization; but for that very reason fall outside the scope of ethnology.

The strains or components of hereditary race and acquired civilization differ not only in number but in the following respect. Nearly every Philippine people can be assigned definitely or at least preponderatingly to this or that race. It is pure Negrito, prevailingly Indonesian, or clearly Malaysian, as the case may be. Only a few small groups are sufficiently intermediate to be classifiable with doubt. But there is no Philippine nationality of which we can say that its civilization is wholly of one stratum. Without exception each tribe has, in its culture, elements belonging to different layers. A people of Mindanao will use the bow, which is perhaps due to Indonesian civilization; the blowgun, which may be of Malaysian source; steel swords, whose manufacture was introduced from India; and firearms which the Mohammedan brought in. A pagan group in Luzon will beat out barkcloth in the manner of its Indonesian ancestors or Negrito predecessors and also weave cotton that came from India; live in a state of society that is native pre-Malaysian, divine the future by methods that originated in Babylonia and were familiar in Rome, and possess pottery and brass imported from China. The Mangyan, a distinctly "wild" people, use the bow which goes back to a pre-iron culture stage, and an alphabet derived from India; the civilized Tagalog read and write Roman letters, wear Europeanized clothes, but continue to live largely in the Malaysian status of society.

In short, then, six to eight separate waves of civilization can be established as having reached the Philippines and left their influence upon the life of the islands. But not one of these successive cultures has been preserved complete. They have been superimposed; but they have interpenetrated one another; until today there is probably not a single nationality but shares in some measure in the effects of every one of the cultures. Civilization reached the Philippines in layers; but the stratification has long since become intricately displaced, nonconformable, and complexly interwoven.

BIBLIOGRAPHY

BARROWS, D. P. A History of the Philippines. Indianapolis, [1905].—A useful little volume, notable for the perspective of its background.

BARTON, R. F. Ifugao Law. (University of California Publications in American Archæology and Ethnology, volume 15, No. 1, Berkeley, 1919.)—The best treatise on this tribe or topic.

Ifugao Economics. (University of California Publications in American Archæology and Ethnology, volume 15, No. 5, Berkeley, 1922.)

BENEDICT, LAURA W. A Study of Bagobo Ceremonial, Magic, and Myth. (Annals, New York Academy of Sciences, volume 25, New York, 1916.)—The most intensive study of Filipino religion yet made.

BEYER, H. OTLEY. Population of the Philippine Islands in 1916. Manila, 1917.—Includes an invaluable little encyclopædia of tribes, and is probably the most important work of reference compiled on Philippine ethnology.

The Philippines before Magellan: I, The Hindus in Malaysia; II, Early Chinese Relations with Malay Lands. (Asia, volume 21, pp. 861–866, 924–928, 1921.)—Illuminating chapters from a prospective book.

BLAIR, E. H., and ROBERTSON, J. A. The Philippine Islands, 1493–1803, volumes 1–55. Cleveland, 1903–1909.—An enormously valuable collection and translation from Spanish sources, containing all the important documents of early ethnology, including the accounts of Magellan, Legazpi, Articda, Chirino, Morga, Combes, etc.

BLUMENTRITT, F. Diccionario Mitológico. (In W. E. Retana, Archivo del Bibliófilo Filipino, volume 2, Madrid, 1896.)

Versuch einer Ethnographie der Philippinen. Gotha, 1882.

CENSUS OF THE PHILIPPINE ISLANDS, 1903, 4 volumes, Washington, 1905.—Volume 1, Geography, History, and Population, is particularly useful.

CHRISTIE, E. B. The Subanuns of Sindangan Bay. (Bureau of Science, Division of Ethnology, volume 6, No. 1, Manila, 1909.)

COLE, F. C. Traditions of the Tinguian. (Field Museum of Natural History, Anthropological Series, volume 14, No. 1, Chicago, 1915.)—The fullest account of the mythology of any one people.

231

COLE, F. C., (continued)
The Wild Tribes of Davao District, Mindanao. (Field Museum of Natural History, Anthropological Series, volume 12, No. 2, Chicago, 1913.)—Best general description of the Mindanao pagans.

The Tinguian. (Field Museum of Natural History, Anthropological Series, volume 14, No. 2, Chicago, 1922.)—An intensive monograph.

COLE, F. C., and LAUFER, B. Chinese Pottery in the Philippines. (Field Museum of Natural History, Anthropological Series, volume 12, No. 1, Chicago, 1912.)

FOLKMAR, D. Album of Philippine Types. Manila, 1904.—Portraits and measurements.

HEINE-GELDERN, R. Südostasien. (In G. Buschan, Illustrierte Völkerkunde, volume 2, pp. 689–968, 1923.)

JENKS, A. E. The Bontoc Igorot. (Ethnological Survey Publications, volume 1, Manila, 1905.)—The most complete general account yet published of any pagan tribe; particularly full on the side of economic life.

LAUFER, B. The Relations of the Chinese to the Philippine Islands. (Smithsonian Miscellaneous Collections, volume 50, Washington, 1907.)

MERRILL, E. D. A Discussion and Bibliography of Philippine Flowering Plants. (Bureau of Science, Popular Bulletin 2, Manila, 1926.) —Much broader than the title. The geological, environmental, biological, and cultural relations of the archipelago are reviewed in the light of recent researches. Plate 3 is a language map, compiled by H. O. Beyer, which modifies maps 4, 5, and 6 of the present volume at many points.

MEYER, A. B. The Distribution of the Negritos in the Philippine Islands and Elsewhere. Dresden, 1899.

MOSS, C. R. Nabaloi Law and Ritual; Kankanay Ceremonies. (University of California Publications in American Archæology and Ethnology, volume 15, Nos. 3 and 4, Berkeley, 1920.)

PHILIPPINE JOURNAL OF SCIENCE. Volumes 1 following, Manila, 1906, following.—To volume 4, anthropology is in Section A, from volume 5 in Section D.

REED, W. A. Negritos of Zambales. (Ethnological Survey Publications, volume 2, No. 1, Manila, 1905.)—Fullest available description of any Negrito group in the islands.

SALEEBY, N. M. Studies in Moro History, Law, and Religion; The History of Sulu. (Bureau of Science, Division of Ethnology, volume 4, Nos. 1, 2, Manila, 1905, 1908.)—Excellent works on the Mohammedans.

SULLIVAN, L. R. Racial Types in the Philippine Islands. (Anthropological Papers, American Museum of Natural History, volume 23, part 1, New York, 1918.)—A complete review of the subject, with reference to all data.

WORCESTER, DEAN C. Headhunters of Northern Luzon. (National Geographic Magazine, volume 23, 1912.)

The Non-Christian Peoples of the Philippine Islands. (National Geographic Magazine, volume 24, 1913.)

The Philippines Past and Present. 2 volumes. New York, 1914.

INDEX

Abaca, cloth, 128; fiber, 95, 97, 128.

Adolescence, ceremonies, not reported, 157.

Adultery, penalty for, 155, 162, 163.

Aesthetic development, meagerness of, 106.

Aeta, 39.

Agriculture, 31, 34, 44, 68, 81–84, 96, 106, 171; acreage devoted to, 97; ceremonies for, 196–197; division of labor in, 153; implements employed in, 35, 92; *kaingin* system of, 31, 87.

Alphabets, Philippine, 71, 215, 216.

Altars, 103, 104, 195.

Altitudes, Philippine peaks, 27.

American influence, on Philippine culture, 67, 229.

Amusements, 61.

Ancestor worship, 188.

Andaman Islands, inhabitants of, 40; language, 42.

Animal, breeding, 82, 95; life, East Indies, 23; sacrifice, 85–86, 161, 166, 167, 204; skins, infrequent use of, 107.

Animals, domesticated, 82, 84; souls attributed to, 192.

Anito, 187–189, 191, 192, 193, 217.

Apayao, 56, 65, 89, 131, 138, 172, 180.

Architecture, 98.

Area, total Philippine, 21; under cultivation, 34.

Areca, cultivation of, 96.

Arithmetical operations, 212.

Armor, 182–185.

Arrow releases, 178.

Arrows, 175–178.

Arson, penalty for, 164.

Art, 217.

Astronomy, 211–212.

Ata, 69.

Ato, institution of, 67, 105, 150.

Augury, 161, 203–205.

Australians, 25, 27.

Austric languages, 80.

Austro-Asiatic languages, 41, 79–80.

Austronesian languages, 79, 80.

Ax, 107, 175, 176.

Babuyanes Islands, 21, 110.

Bagobo, 48, 64, 69, 76, 89, 97, 102, 115, 119, 128, 130, 131, 132, 136, 137, 153, 154, 173, 177, 178, 181, 191, 192, 199, 201, 203, 219.

Bajao, 63.

Bamboo, implements of, 114, 178; use of, 106, 125.

Banana, cultivation of, 95.

Barangay community, 142–145, 150.

Bark cloth, 129, 131, 230.

Barong, 118, 119.

Barrios, 105.

Basket materials, 125, 126.

Baskets, 45, 123–128.

Cire perdue, process of casting, 121.

Civilization, Philippine, complexity of, 226–230; development of, 11–12, 205; stratification of, 12–19, 230.

Clams, as food, 96.

Clans, 149, 150, 151.

Classes, social, 93–94, 147–151.

Climate, Philippine, 27–31.

Cloth, *piña,* 97, 129; trade in, 170; weaving, 97, 128–129, 217.

Clothing, Christian peoples, 61; men's, 129–132; Negrito, 44–45; women's, 137–138.

Coats, 131; women's, 137–138.

Coconut palm, cultivation of, 94.

Codes, law, 68, 141, 157–165.

Coiling, 124, 125–126.

Conquest, Spanish, 13, 31, 61, 63, 144, 170.

Continental affiliations, Philippine Islands, 23–27.

Cooking, 45, 92.

Cotabato, 62.

Cotton, cultivation of, 97–98, 128; weaving of, 230.

Councils, for conducting trials, 158.

Courtship, 153.

Cousin marriage, 156.

Crimes, recognized, fines and restitution for, 157–158.

Crops, cultivation of, 31, 82.

Culture, Indonesian, 226, 227; influences on Philippine, 226–228; Malaysian, 226–227; Negrito, 18–19, 42–47, 226; Philippine, American influences on, 67, 229; Philippine, foreign influences on, 13–18,

205, 226–229; Philippine, general characterization of, 57–71; Southeast Asiatic, 228; stratification of, 12–19, 225.

Culverins, 185.

Dairy products, not utilized, 84.

Dato, 16, 146, 148, 158, 163.

Day, divisions of the, 212.

Death, ceremonies and customs connected with, 101, 133, 134, 166, 197, 201.

Debt of life, 171–175.

Debts, payment and pledges for, 166.

Decoration, personal, 44; pottery, 107–108.

Decorative art, 217.

Descent, reckoning of, 142, 150, 151.

Deutero-Malayan, 49; physical characters, 53.

Dialects, Bisayan, 78–79; local, 75, 78–79.

Disease, cause determined by omen, 200; ceremonies for curing, 196; methods of curing, 200–201; spirits cause of, 199.

Divination, 202–205, 230.

Divorce, 154, 155.

Diwata, 187.

Domestication, of animals, 81–82, 84, 85.

Duels, 160.

Earthquakes, 29, 98, 201.

East Indies, geological and biological areas in, 23; races of the, 26.

Eclipses, beliefs as to causes, 211.